GROUP LIFE

GROUP LIFE

AN INVITATION TO
LOCAL SOCIOLOGY

Gary Alan Fine
Tim Hallett

polity

First published in 2023 by Polity Press

Polity Press
65 Bridge Street
Cambridge CB2 1UR, UK

Polity Press
111 River Street
Hoboken, NJ 07030, USA

ISBN-13: 978-1-5095-5413-3
ISBN-13: 978-1-5095-5414-0 (pb)

A catalogue record for this book is available from the British Library.

Library of Congress Control Number: 2022932972

Typeset in 11 on 13pt Sabon
by Fakenham Prepress Solutions, Fakenham, Norfolk NR21 8NL
Printed and bound in Great Britain by CPI Group (UK) Ltd, Croydon

The publisher has used its best endeavors to ensure that the URLs for external websites referred to in this book are correct and active at the time of going to press. However, the publisher has no responsibility for the websites and can make no guarantee that a site will remain live or that the content is or will remain appropriate.

Every effort has been made to trace all copyright holders, but if any have been overlooked the publisher will be pleased to include any necessary credits in any subsequent reprint or edition.

For further information on Polity, visit our website:
politybooks.com

Make the attempt if you want to, but you will find that trying to go through life without friendship, is like milking a bear to get cream for your morning coffee. It is a whole lot of trouble, and then not worth much after you get it.

– Zora Neale Hurston, *Dust Tracks on a Road*

We dedicate this volume to Zora Neale Hurston and to those friends who traveled with us. Hurston is correct that one can make one's own way, but it is trouble and not worth much. And, so, we owe much to those who read – and critiqued – an earlier draft of this manuscript: Beth Bechky, Ugo Corte, Michaela DeSoucey, Corey Fields, Nahoko Kameo, Lisa Jo van den Scott, and Hannah Wohl.

Contents

Addresses how identities arise from local spaces and, given this focus, the forms that identity takes. From the standpoint of local sociology, identity is neither a personal claim, nor an inevitable result of one's place in a social structure. Rather, identity is linked to affiliation with a web of groups. The presentation of identity depends on two processes: the development of reflective identity, and the embrace of collective identity. In both cases, identity develops from participating in groups and communities, and in recognizing the salience of those connections.

Explores the question of what encourages people to remain in those groups that they choose or in which they are placed. We describe the benefits of participating in a local community. Sociality matters, not only through the immediate pleasures of interaction, but also in the connections of belonging. These connections permit the development of social capital, building relations of trust. By belonging to a group, one can access resources shared by others. These resources not only are material, but include emotional support, the benefits of acquaintanceship, and awareness of novel cultural forms.

Part II   *The World of the Group* 71

Addresses how culture channels group activity. Culture builds group content and simultaneously directs interaction. The chapter describes the concept of idiocultures or local group cultures. While identity and interaction matter in establishing group life, common references and a shared past are crucial to understanding how routines – circuits of action – develop. To be able to know, to use, and then to respond appropriately to a shared set of traditions demonstrates an awareness of, a commitment to, and an inclusion in a group. This permits the local community to shape individual lives and social structures.

Presents the meso-level process by which collective action is possible as a result of tight-knit emotional affiliation. The power of interpersonal bonding demonstrates how individuals organize their behavior to produce desired outcomes and motivate coordinated action. A powerful sense of identity not only shapes the individual but generates collaboration. Social bonds build a commitment to solve problems cooperatively. Believing that members of groups properly belong together justifies joint action in support of a common civic purpose. Sharing a local orientation does not ensure agreement, but it does encourage teamwork.

Part III   *The Group in the World* 121

Addresses conflict and control in local sociology. Groups are not always placid islands; they can generate intense dispute. While smooth interaction may be desired, local communities often contain dissent and disruption. Group stability can be preserved despite participants with divergent interests and values if they agree on the rules by which debate should proceed or can respond effectively to external pressures. Group life can last as long as participants maintain a commitment to their collective identity and a belief in the value of their activities. Within a local community, rivalry can coexist with a desire to maintain relations that encourage orderly interaction.

Recognizes that a focus on groups as the basis of society truncates sociology. Not all social life depends on the local. Despite their significance, groups are linked to more extended communities, and these linkages must be described. The group does not encompass the world, and not all social systems are comprised of freestanding, isolated groups. In contrast, society is built through a web of groups. Groups intersect, and influence spreads as a result. This involves a process of group extension: threads of social relations and beliefs that diffuse throughout a larger population, leading to a consideration of how social media fit into a local sociology.

– 1 –

Believing in Groups: The Possibility of Local Sociology

A nation is the same people living in the same place.

James Joyce, *Ulysses*

At the heart of the writings of James Joyce, arguably the most influential novelist of modernity, are deep and granular depictions of his beloved city of Dublin. Joyce was a master of emphasizing how tiny communities provide a window into the human condition. His magnum opus, *Ulysses*, brims with a multiplicity of groups and connections. Along with its linguistic and literary fireworks, Joyce provides a map of social relations: the novel is a form of social cartography – a travelogue of intimate places. Dublin is the world writ small. As he wrote, "For myself, I always write about Dublin, because if I can get to the heart of Dublin, I can get to the heart of all cities of the world. In the particular is contained the universal." *Ulysses* reveals Dublin's soul through the details of its scenes. Countries and cities, families, faculties, and factories arise from the particular.

In contrast to much sociological writing that focuses on those institutions and structures that stand above – and often apart from – groups and their members, we take inspiration from James Joyce and his focus on the local. A sociology that does not focus on groups is an inadequate and thin discipline. We address this weakness by developing an approach that we label "local sociology." As Eviatar Zerubavel (1997) emphasizes, people belong to "thought communities," but, simultaneously, they belong to action communities. Our vision for local sociology attends to these thought and action communities via a focus on group interaction.

Local sociology is based on the idea that sociology must include *sociality*. It is an oddity of the discipline that many forms of sociological analysis choose to avoid an emphasis on the social. By this, we mean that they ignore the ongoing interactions and group life that constitute lived experience. Our goal in this volume is to demonstrate how a focus on groups, their meanings, the social relations of members, and their intersections provides a valuable approach. This is not the only way to view the world, but it is a perspective that too often is marginalized when sociologists emphasize structure or personal agency.

In focusing on the local, we argue that group life provides a basis by which individuals fit into society and through which social structures shape action. Sociological analysis has been replete with debates about "micro" and "macro," but all too often these arguments miss the point. It is not simply that microsociology provides a foundation for macrosociology, or that macrosociology provides a foundation for microsociology, but that interacting groups are the hinge that connects them. Exploring how groups create social order is our topic. To understand how structures matter and how individuals navigate them, sociologists must watch and listen to groups and people gathering in local communities. We provide an approach that demonstrates how the meso-level of analysis informs both the macro- and micro-levels. This is where the action is.

In the pages that follow, we make the case for local sociology, hoping to expose those who emphasize individual actors or collective entities to the importance of communities of interaction. Of course, the pieces of our argument are not new. We have been developing this approach for decades. Further, this is an approach with a lengthy pedigree in sociology and that resonates with many sociological classics, even if it has never been the dominant model.

This text is a work of synthesis, a compact account of a level of analysis that treats interaction and culture as central. Although we present new material, we draw on research by Gary Alan Fine in his previous books, *Tiny Publics: A Theory of Group Action and Culture* (Fine 2012) and *The Hinge: Civil Society, Group Cultures, and the Power of Local Commitments* (Fine 2021). While hoping for a wide audience, we write primarily for the committed graduate student or advanced undergraduate major who desires an overview of how to think about social order apart from assuming a dominant role of either the individual or the society, a theoretical approach that is distinct from cognitive hegemony or structural supremacy.

Beyond the "Macro" and the "Micro"

The discipline of sociology has long been split over the choice of which analytic level is most valuable, and, it must be admitted, justifications exist for each choice. People and structures will always constitute society, and we do not dismiss either. Sociologists, with their training and their preferences, study what they feel is crucial, and they do it well. As a discipline, we benefit from pluralist lenses, but each way of seeing is also a way of not seeing. Many sociologists argue that the field's core concerns how institutions, states, and global systems have effects, channeling and constraining personal options. In this vision, individuals and interaction are confined to the margins. Perhaps we might describe this as a social science that avoids the social. In contrast, others examine how persons respond, elevating a social psychology, a world of selves, buffeted by the institutional. These scholars focus on interpersonal relations, identity, and selves as they affect individuals, but at times they ignore what people do together and how those interactions matter. In a sense, they, too, avoid the social. Our task is to bring these scholars together on the grounds of the social without dismissing either the personal or the institutional.

These two groups of scholars have been labeled Macros and Micros. This division became so solidified that several decades ago some theorists demanded a "Micro–Macro Link" (Alexander et al. 1987), a bandage intended to bind a sociological wound. Individual action – what was described as agency – might, in this view, coexist with institutional structure. Consensus emerged that such a connection was necessary and essential, but its acceptance often rested on a pragmatic reality that the perspectives developed under a protective, if hypothetical, umbrella: a big tent sociology that would let scholars go their own way.

These alternate approaches miss a crucial point. Participation in groups is central to the shaping of identity. That we belong to local communities – and treasure them – provides a grounding that permits us to commit ourselves to building and preserving the world around us as experienced. From this, we argue that joint action is central to society, and that groups are the quintessential sites where people act together. Sociology should theorize this joint action as central to how society is possible. To appreciate the influences of structures and individuals is to recognize how they are connected. To move beyond the limits of the Micro–Macro meme, local sociology recognizes groups as essential for developing a meso-level of analysis that stands between the individual and larger structures (Turner 2005). This approach constitutes the nexus of a full sociology.

Treating the group as a central organizing principle claims that it is metaphorically both a *crucible* and a *hinge*.

Local communities are crucibles in that much change and solidarity occur within bounded spaces. These spaces can generate heat and conflict. But they are also hinges in that the group provides a semi-autonomous and flexible means of joining micro and macro. "Crucible" and "hinge" are companion tropes that characterize local sociology. We emphasize the place of engagement (the crucible) and the linkage of levels of analysis (the hinge).

In focusing on groups and communities, local sociology values those methodologies that rely on keen vision, close listening, and precise description: these are our disciplinary birthright. Sociology is a field that thrives *in place*: in the kitchens, parks, taverns, and offices of Dublin, Dubai, Chicago, Chennai, Hong Kong, and Addis Ababa. And currently on Facebook, TikTok, Twitter, and Tinder. Honoring local action, observations open windows of understanding. Accounts of what people do and say are inevitably limited in that they present a particular event to reveal more frequent occurrences. This constitutes sociological synecdoche, transforming anecdote into theory. The willingness to report what one witnessed relies on the claim that the particular can be generalized, revealing wider or deeper meanings. Seeing is believing – and persuading. Specifics stand for a panoply of similar events. If audiences judge the account as plausible or if they have had comparable experiences, they treat it as reflecting a widespread practice. Our approach to meso-level theorizing considers ethnographic observation especially amenable to the group-level analysis that justifies local sociology.

To treat the world as social space, we must recognize that groups – their cultures and their dynamic processes – shape who we are, how we behave, and what we believe. When groups change, voluntarily or through pressure, individuals are altered as well. In short, the communities with which we identify and people with whom we associate direct our practices, both those that are routine and those that are creative. We reside in a world of tiny publics, or, in the language of Alexis de Tocqueville, a crowd of *minute associations*.

One advantage of examining groups is the many cases from which one can draw. Each group provides an observable reality. We have numerous accounts of what the great Polish-American sociologist Florian Znaniecki (1940) spoke of as social circles, with their associated rights, roles, and rules. These include friendship cliques, artistic cenacles, political clubs, work teams, communes, scientific laboratories, gangs, and social movements. From teams of scientists in Antarctica to local Klaverns of the Ku Klux Klan, from the French Impressionists to surfers, from Girl Scout troops to the president's National Security team, groups fulfill our desires for sociability, for identity, for change, and for status. Human life is group life, a cross-cultural reality that defines our humanity and suggests the centrality of interaction for any social science that hopes to explain the world as lived. Separation from others is emotionally devastating, explaining why the COVID-19 lockdowns have caused many to feel less human. We yearn for shared environs that make us whole.

Our goal is to explicate that space – the hinge – between the individual and the institution. This is where sets of individuals *together* shape meaning, separate from what has been institutionally given, and create collective identity, separate from self and demography. Group cultures both shape individual commitments and permit the building of extended systems of constraint. The linkage of groups – small but consequential publics – provides the basis for social order.

By examining community close up and treating it as revealing patterns of relations, we build a local sociology beyond selves or realms: this is a world of joint action, a world of people doing things together (Becker 1986). Of course, in any study, the questions asked determine the proper level of analysis. Every project attempts to answer an open sociological question, and some questions can be answered without attending to group dynamics. Minute communities do not stand opposed to other forms of analysis, but require recognition of self and structure. We celebrate the diversity of sociology by formulating an approach that recovers and builds on longstanding traditions, arguing that, for a social science to thrive, at its root it must be social.

The Light of Sociability: The (Unmet) Promise of Group Theory

In describing the structure of intellectual networks in sociology, Nicholas Mullins (1973) labeled Small Group Theory as "the light that failed." This was an ironic description of a tradition to which his own analysis of "theory groups" contributed. Small Group Theory was an approach to which the 1954 *American Sociological Review* devoted a rare special issue, but which had started to be marginalized by the time of Mullins' analysis, a result of developments in cognitive science and in structural analysis (Steiner 1974; Hackman and Katz 2010). Sociologists struggled to extend group dynamics to core questions of the discipline (Collins 1999).

In place of examining ongoing social relations, structural models have dominated sociology, and cognitive models of individual action have dominated psychology. And yet the study of ongoing, self-referential, close-knit groups remains crucial to examining how affiliation, community, and culture are generated. In fact, theorists are well aware of the field-defining contributions of such influential figures as Georg Simmel, George Herbert Mead, George Homans, Tamotsu Shibutani, Charles Horton Cooley, Helena Lopata, and Erving Goffman. Together these figures and their many contemporary avatars engaged the discipline by emphasizing that groups, sociality, and behavior were central to social organization. The domain of interaction solves a set of sociological problems that otherwise remain opaque. Foregrounding groups demystifies the longstanding puzzle of how structures have effects. Groups and extended networks provide domains in which participants respond to the world around them and contribute to joint projects that shape that world.

By using the term "group," we refer to an aggregation of persons characterized by mutual awareness, shared place, common identity, collective culture, interpersonal relations, mutual commitment, and understood routines. Not all sets of actors have these characteristics or reveal them continually. However, these features are the basis of group life, be those groups admirable or not. These micro-communities reveal how status, inequality, and biases operate in practice. Despite the allegiances that groups prize and often celebrate, they also may develop hierarchies that at times and in places can be unbending.

Participants know each other as discrete persons or through their personas: their positions or reputations. Community members strive for a recognizable set of common interests or concerns, and they share beliefs in what constitutes decorum and propriety, which in its behavioral form constitutes norms. These norms, when embraced, provide a sense of unity or we-ness (Tuomela 2007), leading to rarely questioned relations of trust. We consider traditional primary groups (family), secondary groups (workgroups, cliques, or voluntary associations), online forums, and ephemeral groups that gather for a moment and dissipate after their shared experience ends.

While the number of participants helps to define a *small* group, there are no precise numerical limits. Instead, the small group refers to a set of persons who recognize each other as belonging to an interdependent community. Robert Freed Bales (1950: 33), a leading social psychologist who devoted his lengthy career to describing the dynamics of self-analytic groups, defines a small group as "any number of persons engaged in interaction with each other in a single face-to-face meeting or series of meetings, in which each member receives some impression or perception of each other member distinct enough so that he can, either at the time or in later questioning, give some reaction to each of the others as an individual person." Bales' approach recognizes that belonging is crucial, tied to the presence of collective identity. Identity construction occurs over time, even if the participants do not consciously recognize local structure, culture, conflict, and trust.

Although much research on groups has emphasized face-to-face interaction, groups may also operate through online, digital, or telephonic communication. Whatever the form, the action and response typically have temporal immediacy. Admittedly, this model of group life may discount disagreement and divergence, important phenomena that we address in chapter 6. Nevertheless, groups exist despite – and because of – conflict so long as participants hold the disruption of the quotidian in check by committing to continuing participation. On some occasions, disruptions solidify allegiance by revealing the stakes and setting the stage for conflicts that, although fraught, provide recognizable positions and become the basis for predictable interaction (Tavory and Fine 2020).

When groups build consensus, social order is possible (Brint 2001). Of course, conflict and disruptions may also be generated, but that, too, reveals the importance of mutual awareness. Regardless, when we assume the salience of a drive toward consensus, recurring, meaningful, self-referential interaction provides for stability and collective identity. Social structures depend for their tensile strength on the existence of groups with shared pasts and imagined futures, that are spatially situated, that create identification, and that desire to preserve enduring relations (Fine 2012). In contrast to those who claim that order is constantly constructed anew in each interaction scene (a complaint commonly made of ethnomethodology and dramaturgical analysis), meso-communities – like those in Joyce's Dublin – establish a solid sense of identity and organization. These are performative spaces, but the performances have recognizable scripts that guide the expectations of participants. Shared understandings that arise from continuing interaction provide the cultural basis for action, a point emphasized by Erving Goffman (1983) in depicting the *interaction order.*

Thinking in this way, the group becomes a crucible in which individuals together align their actions and apply their shared identities to link to larger communities, just as the social control that emanates from larger communities motivates, encourages, or constrains group action. In this sense, we speak of groups and society as being *mutually constitutive.* Society can be treated as an ecology – or a network – of groups. Groups are rarely isolated, and they are knit together in complex patterns, strong or fragmentary. In any complex society, the groups that exist intersect with each other, and may share members. Further, they participate in more extended community cultures. Overlapping like fish-scales, they borrow traditions. This allows for a spread of influence as groups abut each other and transmit values, norms, and beliefs. This reality forces us to recognize that the image of the isolated pod is insufficient for a robust sociology. We reside in a network of groups (Fine and Kleinman 1979).

The reality that groups engage with each other makes an extended organizational life possible. Organizations survive not only because of the formal arrangement of personnel, but also through the interaction scenes that these arrangements generate, where many groups populate the same organizational environment. Organizations are inhabited, and, as a result, become powerful action realms (Hallett 2010; Hallett and Ventresca 2006).

Although culture, interaction, and structure are central to any model that links levels of analysis, those concepts in themselves are too broad for theorizing. Too much can be treated as culture, interaction, or structure. While the intersection of these concepts serves as the basis of a meso-level sociology, integrating action and order, specific themes permit us to see how civic order results from communal practices. To realize the unmet promise of group theory, we draw on four concepts that, while they overlap, address the linkage of micro- and macro- through the precedence of meso-level analysis: the interaction order, circuits of action, group cultures, and tiny publics.

The Interaction Order

Our focus on groups extends Erving Goffman's (1983) influential account of the interaction order. Goffman argued that interaction is orderly, even while recognizing the agentic choices of participants. Communities create standards for appropriate action. In the public display of these standards, performances solidify social order. This process is inherent in his dramaturgical model, which built on a theatrical metaphor (Brissett and Edgley 2017). People do not merely think and behave; they perform for others in a staged attempt to manage impressions and, often, smooth over disputes.

However, Goffman's concern throughout much of his writing is to examine those moments in which the parties are not in extended, meaningful contact. He often emphasizes fleeting encounters, such as those between clerks and customers, while only gesturing to the presence of other "deeper" relations that depend on biographic awareness and local cultures.

We are less concerned with fleeting encounters in contrast to the interaction orders of ongoing groups. While we recognize the importance of Goffman's argument that the interaction order operates in its own right with distinctive properties, people believe in and respond to the seemingly obdurate qualities of social structures. Shared practices arise from the repetition of similar types of encounters. Both action and meaning are incorporated into the lifeworlds of community members, contributing to a feeling of normality. While social order depends on the traditions and the standards of societies and subcultures, what we refer to as an *interaction* order emphasizes the salience of local action spaces.

Every interaction order builds on a shared, communal past. Allegiance to these pasts provides a *commitment mechanism* that encourages participation in group life. In the strong case, communal affiliation shapes an actor's identity, becoming a marker of self and of belonging. In the weak case, affiliation establishes a tacit desire to follow what influential colleagues define as proper. Since every act occurs within a limited context, recognizing these contexts as sites for interpretation and action is central to local sociology.

Of course, the immediate encounter does not, by itself, establish a collective relation, but, rather, the collective relation depends on repeated and repeatable patterns of action. In treating our experience of past interaction as a model for the present, recognizing our ability to compare and contrast contexts, society is built through a tacit agreement to transform action into order. Interaction rituals serve as the basis for trust at all levels (Misztal 2001): from the dyad to the crowd, and from the bedroom to the state.

Our approach recognizes an upsurge of interest in processes that recognize the emergent, the brokered, the attached, and the embedded. By emphasizing the context of action, we underscore how meanings and relations provide epistemic stability and intersubjectivity, allowing for shared expectations that flow from common experiences. The range of active research topics that acknowledge the importance of local contexts is large, and includes emergent mechanisms of cause-and-effect (Sawyer 2005), socially embedded and networked brokerage (Hillmann 2008), emotional attachments to nested groups (Lawler, Thye, and Yoon 2009), local structures that shape identity (Bearman 1991), dual-process models (Vaisey 2009), the locational resources shaping creative performance (Corte 2013), and the spatial conditions of scientific discovery (Parker and Hackett 2012).

These research domains, distinct in method, substance, and theory, appreciate the power of local contexts. A particularly compelling example is found in the neighborhood effects literature. This research demonstrates that broad structural forces do not by themselves shape personal outcomes. Rather, they are mediated through the culture of one's home turf. Variables such as collective efficacy depend on the form and the history of continuing group relations, as not all poor communities produce the same outcomes (Sampson, Morenoff, and Gannon-Rowley 2002). As David Harding (2010) suggests in his examination of poor neighborhoods in Boston, in order to understand neighborhood effects, one must recognize the impact of cliques, relationships, and cultures.

The importance of interaction orders is evident in a wide array of domains, including juries as local systems for generating justice (Diamond and Rose 2005; Burnett 2001), congregations as sites for the display of faith (Becker 1999; Chen 2002; Putnam and Campbell 2010), family and relationships as points of obligation (Oring 1984; Bendix 1987), neighborhoods as generators of habitual activity (Grannis 2009), and work teams as culture carriers (Lipman-Blumen and Leavitt 2001; Sparrowe et al. 2001). These minute associations are not always efficient or collegial (Kaufmann 2009; Weeks 2003), but they support social order as they provide the comforts of ongoing relations.

Circuits of Action

The ordering of interaction is stressed in Erving Goffman's (1983: 4) comment that "at the very center of interaction life is the cognitive relation we have with those present before us, without which relationship our activity, behavioral and verbal, could not be meaningfully organized." By participating in an interaction order, group members recognize that their associations and their practices are stable, but this stability demands to be considered in its own right. Stability does not emerge from the immediate encounter but is the outcome of a set of *routines* that develop from ongoing social relations.

We describe these routines as revealing the dynamic properties of groups, which we label circuits of action (Fine 2021). That we describe them as circuits suggests that these actions are performed not merely for themselves, but as a *pathway* to further responses: an established itinerary that members understand as part of a larger sequence of routines. Social order could barely exist without predictable sequences of behavior. When linked together, they become the kind of interaction ritual chains described by Randall Collins (2004).

Circuits of action place routine practices as central to local sociology; the concept emphasizes that routines are not only linked to individuals, but part of a desire for sociality, and are responded to as such. They address culturally appropriate reactions to ongoing constraints. In this, interaction is filtered through the awareness of what participants collectively believe is appropriate. We can think of this as extending principles of decorum. In other words, circuits of action mirror the expectations of the interaction order and the content of local cultures in generating predictable action. They are guides to behavior: self-help strategies for living a group life. However, these are not laws or demands. For interaction to be predictable within a collaborative group, adjustments are essential. Symbolic interactionists such as Anselm Strauss (1978) and David Maines (1977) point to negotiation as a tool for building flexible but durable relations, not built afresh at each moment but operating within a pre-existing context. A meaningful, referential past exists on which participants rely to create their futures. Ultimately, people act socially because they expect others to act similarly. Instead of being composed of individuals with distinct minds, groups are comprised of common practices, making coordination possible.

Group Cultures
Circuits of action highlight the importance of ongoing routines, but they leave the role of culture implicit, as if

group life was devoid of meaning. This is never the case, as group life requires content. Behavior is almost always *about* something, even if that "something" is tacit. The presence of group cultures suggests that culture is more than simply an amorphous mist (Ghaziani 2009). Instead, it consists of a set of beliefs and practices held by those with continuing and valued relations. While some traditions are widespread, others are highly localized. Still, whatever the extent of their diffusion, cultural awareness provides a template of activity.

Central to the meso-level perspective is the presence of an idioculture. We define idioculture as "a system of knowledge, beliefs, behaviors, and customs shared by members of an interacting group to which members can refer and that serve as the basis of further interaction. Members recognize that they share experiences, and these experiences can be referred to with the expectation that they will be understood by other members, thus being used to construct a social reality for the participants" (Fine 1987: 125).

Recognizing that one's experience is shared and can be referred to contributes to a robust identity and sense of belonging. Once group members realize that they hold meaning in common, this understanding can encourage allegiance or produce a demand for change. A recent and dramatic example of this process involves accounts of sexual harassment or assault in the #MeToo or #TimesUp movement. These activists were mobilized through discussions (once labeled "consciousness raising" sessions), face-to-face and now frequently online. Such conversations revealed the frequency of affronts and assaults. But, more than demonstrating the extent of the problem, discourse allowed wider communication within networks and later through media accounts, creating and then reinforcing support, identity, and belonging.

As numerous ethnographies demonstrate, families, teams, clubs, and cliques develop group cultures. The rules and expectations of interaction provide a local community with a belief that the fate of members is joined. While demographic categories also have linked fates (Dawson 1995), members of local communities find their prospects tightly bound. Their linked fates are easily discernible. Ann Swidler (1986) has emphasized that culture operates as a toolkit with strategies available to promote engagement. The collective past and the prospective future define groups. Culture is known through action and, as a result, we emphasize performance, transactions, and coordination (Jasper 2010; Brissett and Edgley 2017). Seeing meaning from the standpoint of the actors recognizes the salience of conduct, rituals, routines, and practices. Common discourses produce a civic imagination, shaped by social location, personal and political experience, and tradition (Baiocchi et al. 2014: 69).

One of the most profound research projects that demonstrates the power of group culture is the Robbers' Cave experiment, conducted by Muzafer Sherif and his colleagues at the University of Oklahoma. They organized a preadolescent summer camp to examine the development and subsequent diminishment of conflict by analyzing the newly formed "traditions" of two cabins of campers. The camp setting encouraged the boys to create nicknames, songs, and jokes. One cabin labeled themselves Eagles; the other, Rattlers. The researchers then set activities in which the two groups competed, where only one could gain rewards. Sherif and his colleagues demonstrated that the rivalry solidified each local culture and promoted hostility to their rivals in battles over resources, reflected in contrasting collective identities. The power of belonging overwhelmed the individual personalities of these children.

The final stage of the research was to create conditions in which the groups overcame their hostile cultures through situations that provided a set of superordinate goals and demanded collaboration. On these occasions, the two cabins were motivated to work together (fixing the camp water supply and deciding on a movie to watch together) (Sherif et al. 1961). The findings demonstrate that a theory of the local must address how traditions respond to collective interests and how those traditions shape responses to novel situations. That interaction is always about *something* – about meaningful content – emphasizes that idiocultures are not random sites of interaction.

Tiny Publics

While all social domains teach us about society, sociologists have a mission to examine the development of community awareness. Groups, at least those that are influential, are not isolated. Rather, they often have a civil consciousness. When groups address a broader politics, we speak of them as *tiny publics*, a community with an idioculture that contributes to civil society. While this is not always true, the concept of a tiny public reflects the reality that numerous groups develop an implicit politics and present a communal face that is outward looking. These worlds may be small, but they are the lifeblood of civil society, found on street corners and in global corporate boardrooms.

Analyzing tiny publics opens a window into the dynamics of political engagement. The American philosopher John Dewey (1954: 42) explained this in his influential treatise *The Public and Its Problems*, writing: "The intimate and familiar propinquity group is not a social unity within an inclusive whole. It is, for almost all purposes, society itself." For Dewey's civic pragmatism, the "propinquity group" [the tiny public] constitutes society with knowledge interpreted socially. This supports Dewey's clever metaphor that, in democracies, the ear is more powerful than the eye: communication among colleagues matters more than what any one individual can observe. Dewey (1954: 218–19) writes, "Vision is a spectator; hearing is a participator." Ears learn of public morality, whereas eyes only require an internal compass.

While tiny publics are at the heart of Dewey's view of democracy, they are also found in authoritarian systems.

These groups may stand opposed to totalizing systems, but this is not inevitable (Riley 2010). We must not assume that groups are nice by nature, or that they are necessarily committed to freedom, justice, or equality. Our model does not presume a happy vision of consensual or democratic publics. Groups do not inevitably stand against structures that are more powerful; instead, they may stand with them, buttressing power, privilege, and oppression. We must not assign groups virtue simply because of their modest size (Kaplan 2018: 53). Likewise, while civil society demands a measure of consensus, at least for decision-making, conflict is rarely entirely absent. Tiny publics may split or they may battle others. Civic vice may be as present as civic virtue. We recognize the presence – and occasionally the merits – of conflict and disruption without presuming the inevitable desirability of accord. Seen as a crucible, group action can bubble and burn, but the heat also transforms and creates opportunities. Returning to the research of Muzafer Sherif, the challenge is to create conditions that allow people to recognize the advantages of collaboration.

Part of the challenge faced by a society composed of tiny publics is that, because smooth interaction is embraced as desirable, groups may become conflict-averse, avoiding controversies that might productively be addressed, or simply bowing to the demands of the most powerful. Political scientist Jane Mansbridge (1980: 34), in speaking of "adversary democracy," warns of the danger of consensus:

> When citizens have a common interest, face-to-face contact – which allows debate, empathy, listening, learning, changing opinions, and a burst of solidarity when a decision is reached – can bring real joy. But in the face of conflict, emotions turn sour. . . . Fear of conflict leads those with influence in a meeting to suppress important issues rather than letting them surface and cause disruption. It leads them also to

avoid the appearance of conflict by pressing for unanimity.

Following the imagery of a Quaker meeting, groups often believe that they must embrace harmony and suppress dissent. Too much conflict can be seen as pathological. However, enshrining a single voice as a desirable model potentially silences healthy, if robust, debate.

An array of tiny publics suggests that affiliation need not end at the boundary of interaction but can extend to connections with other groups felt to have similar character. This is especially true because individuals often affiliate with several groups, creating, in effect, a vast patchwork from the fabric of tiny publics. Local cultures are knit into subcultures. Once this broader civic affiliation is recognized, actions – such as voting, contributing, or demonstrating – generate a more consequential set of commitments and identities. These choices contribute to the search for a "good society," a flowering of mutual respect and moral virtue (Bellah et al. 1991). This sunny imaginary stems from a belief that the strong ties of family, friendship, and neighborhood can be extended through caring communities: villages in the interaction order. Still, caring communities can become vicious when their values are threatened from within or beyond. Yet there often remains a local glue even if the community is internally split or has disputed boundaries – a culture of complaint (Weeks 2003) – as long as participants feel that resources, beliefs, or colleagues are worth disputing.

These ruptures remind us that good societies need good publics. Political theorist Michael Walzer (1992: 107) argues: "Civil society itself is sustained by groups much smaller than the *demos* or the working class or the mass of consumers or the nation. All these are necessarily pluralized as they are incorporated. They become part of the fabric of family, friends, comrades and colleagues, where people are connected to one another and made responsible for one another." For Walzer, civil society depends on a network of tiny publics. A good life is possible only in a civil society of sociable members who freely associate and communicate. This is what tiny publics can achieve at their best, and what Robert Putnam (2000), with his provocative metaphor of "Bowling Alone," frets are in decline – a decline that he asserts could threaten democracy. The idea of tiny publics builds on a political sociology that recognizes that a range of publics – elites, conformers, the marginal, and the resistant – each develop from the meanings, social relations, and structures of close-knit communities.

Understanding the Local

The interaction order, circuits of action, group culture, and tiny publics are threads that we weave throughout our tapestry. Building on these strands – our core concepts – each chapter examines a topic through which we conceptualize group life in a way that undergirds local sociology. These topics constitute the knitting of a meso-level social order. Although our approach owes much to the symbolic interactionist tradition, it incorporates aspects of dramaturgy, relational sociology, network analysis, critical realism, and institutionism. We emphasize how communities – recognizable collections of actors – organize themselves through collective meaning making and shared narration.

To justify how a local, interactional, group-based sociology has value, we organize this book around six topics whereby a meso-level focus contributes to understanding social order, while recognizing the role of individuals and structures. We divide our chapters into three yoked pairs. The first pair focuses on *the individual in the group*, the second on *the world of the group*, and the last on *the group in the world*. In each chapter, we emphasize social relations, shared meaning, and spatial connections. In structuring the book, we begin by examining how groups shape selves through identity (being in groups) and through social relations (belonging to groups). We then address how groups serve as sites for the creation of shared meaning, establishing group culture (building groups) and collective action (bonding by groups). Finally, we describe the extended power of groups, revealing how groups engage in boundary-making processes, banding against outsiders, balancing conflict and control (battling groups), and how groups are integrated within extended social networks (bridging groups).

Rather than relying on theory and on speculation alone, we tie our arguments to empirical ethnographic research, which we describe as "thinking in cases." We draw on data from the authors' ethnographic projects, selecting two relevant studies for each chapter as a means to explicate the chapter's themes. Because the studies were conducted prior to this book for other purposes, not all topics in each chapter are considered in these cases, but we hope that the ethnographic forays address the topics in valuable ways. Further, these inserts – as diverse as the groups are in their activities – are limited by those sites that we studied. The groups are largely White middle-class American sites, and the authors are White middle-class men. We are sensitive to this reality, and recognize that the types of groups and the characteristics of their members shape our analysis. There is a trade-off in relying on our own research on groups and not on research into groups that we do not know, but we take heart in the truth that no word is the last word; no book is the last book.

In chapter 2, "Being in Groups," we begin our exploration of a local, group-based, interaction-inspired social theory by asking: from what spaces do identities arise, and what are the key forms that identity takes? In responding to these questions, we examine how actors define themselves. Identity is not merely a personal designation, nor is it automatically provided by one's place within a social structure. In contrast, it is tied to affiliation with groups and to participation in them. As such, understanding identity in light of local sociology depends on two processes: the development of reflective identity, and the embrace of collective identity. Both are activated and motivated in a social context, but they operate in distinct ways. Yet, in both cases, the self-definitional process does not prioritize the individual. Rather, it reflects the power of belonging to communities, but also, crucially, the salience of recognizing that connection.

Sociologists have written much about how identities shape individuals. These identities provide an imagined link to domains of mass society, including the nation, race, religion, gender, ethnicity, and sexual orientation. This belief in affiliation with broad, extra-local identities may downplay seeing oneself in a local context. Institutions, organizations, and subcultural groupings shape our lives in compelling ways. Identities are more than just ideas that people hold. Rather, they must be activated through spaces of interaction. Although exposure to media and participation in mass gatherings can provoke identity activation, it is often within social circles that one's identity is bolstered, extended, and challenged. These scenes demand that individuals consider what identity means in light of the identities of associates. In turn, identity becomes part of a field of interpretation, increasing its influence as a result. To explore this process, we draw upon ethnographic studies of Master of Fine Arts students, and students receiving Master's degrees in public affairs.

People may participate in groups for a host of reasons, but what compels them to *remain* in groups? The answer is found in the benefits of participation in a local community, which is the focus of chapter 3, "Belonging to Groups." Sociality matters, not only in terms of the immediate pleasures of interaction, but also for the connections fostered through belonging. This provides what has been labeled "social capital": the plethora of resources made available through networked relations of trust. By belonging, one can access the resources made available by others. These are not only material, but include emotional support, valuable weak ties (including friends of friends), and exposure to novel cultural tastes. What is crucial, we argue, is not simply engaging in a particular space, but the belief that belonging carries meaning beyond the mere fact of embodied presence. Here we describe the commitment involved in belonging to two teams: staff working in restaurant kitchens, and students participating in high school debate squads.

Together, this pair of chapters focuses on the individual's relationship to the group, treating the community as a source of identity. The next pair focuses on how culture has consequences for the community. Groups generate shared knowledge that secures togetherness.

Chapter 4, "Building Groups," deals with the question of what channels group activity. Culture builds shared knowledge and is the structure that directs ongoing interactions. We emphasize those sociological traditions that are linked to social relations, elaborating on the concept of *idiocultures* that we introduced above. While identity and interaction matter in creating group life, common references and a shared past are crucial to understanding how circuits of action are possible. These aspects of idioculture are necessary for embracing and accepting routine. To know, to use, and to respond appropriately to an integrated set of traditions demonstrates awareness of, commitment to, and inclusion in a group. To illustrate how groups are built, we draw on ethnographic research on Little League baseball teams, and fantasy role-play gamers – worlds of leisure, but ones with structures that permit the establishment of domains of meaning.

In chapter 5, we discuss the meso-level process by which collective action is possible, considering "Bonding by Groups." Bonding addresses how individuals collectively organize their behavior to produce desired outcomes and motivate coordinated action. Identity addresses not merely how an individual selects and embraces a self-definition (chapter 2), but how this self-definition encourages collaboration. As Alexis de Tocqueville recognized in discussing minute communities, these bonds build a desire to solve problems cooperatively. Tocqueville used this characteristic of American towns to explain how knots of citizens could solve problems without relying on power from above. Feeling that residents properly belong together justifies joint action in support of a common civic purpose. Sharing a local orientation does not ensure agreement, but it does justify teamwork. To understand bonding, we draw on two ethnographies, which examine how the spaces of amateur mushroom collectors and senior citizen activists develop organizational bonding and collective action.

The final two substantive chapters explore how boundaries operate inside and outside of groups. Chapter 6, "Battling Groups," asks what the place of conflict and control is in local sociology. In dealing with the question, we recognize that groups are not islands of calm in roiling seas of dispute; they can include volcanic dispute in themselves. While smooth interaction may be desired, local communities handle both dissent and disruption. Group stability can be preserved despite participants with divergent interests and values as long as they agree on a process of debate and discussion, or can coalesce if needing to respond to external pressures. Group life can continue if participants maintain a commitment to their collective identity and a belief in the value of their activities.

In other cases, forms of control, whether desirable or oppressive, are evident. These might bind members together, but, on some occasions, groups split or even contend with competitors. Nevertheless, it is often the case that, within a local community, rivalry can coexist with a commitment to bolster relations that encourage orderly interaction. We explore how conflict can be maintained while not destroying the features that permit us to recognize a shared reality and those forces of control that help to preserve it. To illustrate these processes, we rely on research detailing turmoil within a public elementary school, and the presence of control that shapes government meteorological offices.

To a skeptical reader, a focus on groups is simply too narrow. "Local" as an adjective for sociology might be seen as insulting, proposing a puny discipline. Such skepticism raises the questions of how groups are linked to more extended systems, and what the implications of those linkages are? These questions form the core of chapter 7, "Bridging Groups," which addresses the reality that not all social life is local. The group does not encompass the world, and not all worlds are comprised of free-standing, isolated groups. Our sociological mission is to explore how society is constituted through a network of tiny publics. Communities combine, and influence transfers from one to the next. This constitutes *group extension*: social relations and belief in commonalities that spread throughout a larger population. The diffusion of beliefs, norms, and practices depends on recognized spaces of interaction. While useful, a network model may ignore that people often treat macro-structures as having an obdurate character that cannot merely be reduced to shared activity. When structures are believed to be real, they will be treated as real in action. Whether or not action is inevitably local, it is not always treated as such. To explore this process of bridging, we describe research on communities of folk art collectors and of competitive chess players, both situated in widely dispersed networks.

As noted, our presentation is a work of synthesis. Our goal is to provide a concise case for a sociology that focuses on the group and that is grounded on a meso-level of analysis. As a result, some materials from previous articles, presentations, and books have been incorporated into this account. While there has been considerable rewriting and rethinking, many of these ideas have been presented in other forums. We hope that, by bringing these ideas together, the value of a local approach to studying society will be evident.

Together, these chapters develop a sociology that embraces core concerns by treating the routines and the expectations of interaction seriously. This is a world in which life is ordered through the relations among social actors. Who we know, what we believe, where we act, when we gather, and how we communicate depend on the bedrock reality that we act jointly and that we care about our tiny publics. We do things together. Social life depends not on minnows following in the wake of Leviathans, but rather on the creativity of schools of fish in our watery worlds. This focus leads to our conclusion, chapter 8, "Better Sociology: A Call to Small Arms." Here we articulate seven premises to guide local sociology in hopes that others will follow our inspiration, or will at least recognize and admire the attempt.

– PART I –
THE INDIVIDUAL IN THE GROUP

– 2 –
Being in Groups: Reflective and Collective Identities

The world is a looking-glass. . . . Frown at it, and it
will in turn look sourly upon you; laugh at it and with
it, and it is a jolly kind companion.

William Makepeace Thackeray, *Vanity Fair*

Identity, the presentation of selves to publics, is the entry
point for sociologists to treat persons as performers. But
these are never solo shows. For local sociology, identity
is a feature not only of the isolated individual, but of the
individual in a social surround. As George Herbert Mead
(1934) emphasized in *Mind, Self, and Society*, selves
develop from the interactions that we have with others, be
they colleagues, friends, relatives, or rivals.

While one can reasonably examine how identities arise
from individual experience and personal desires, and
can recognize that identities are the outcome of ascribed
features awarded through the power of broader societal
categories, this is not our intention. We put aside psychological effects – the Freudian experiences that shape our
selves – as well as downplaying the recognition that
collective identities can derive from demographic segments
or large communities, even while realizing that categories

such as race, religion, or gender matter greatly. We deny neither the macro nor micro bases of identity, but in laying out a theory of *local* sociology, we emphasize the meso-level: how selves and their associated identities (internal beliefs and public performances) arise from social contact. In arguing for a group-based sociology, we assert that neither idiosyncratic experience nor categorical position is sufficient. We advocate for a *sociology of identification* that considers the spaces from which identity derives and the forms that it takes.

Identity involves a recognition of belonging. In this way, groups become, in effect, the baptismal font for identity. Identity springs from being in shared spaces, whether located in a home, a park, a workplace, a street corner, an online website, or a church. This is how local sociology connects the meanings of selves to those looking-glasses emphasized, in literature, by Thackeray and, later, in sociology, by Charles Horton Cooley. To claim an identity – a presentation of public selfhood – demands an attachment to organized sociality, treating the evaluations of others as crucial. A performed identity – and not merely a private feeling of selfhood – requires placing oneself in a map of relations. Others may accept those selves or may reject them, particularly if one is seen as outside the communal boundary, but, whether accepted by others or not, the claim must be meaningful for its maker.

"Identity" has come to have many meanings – some suggest too many – as conflicting theories have proliferated (Brubaker and Cooper 2000). Reclaiming the idea of identity for local sociology, we emphasize the linkage between a sense of self and an overt commitment to those groups to which one belongs. Identity is not merely a characteristic of the individual, nor is it the defining and categorical feature of a constraining structure, but, in contrast, identity derives from identification.

From this perspective, it is not either cognition or emotion alone that defines the person. Rather, identities depend on interaction within influential communities that serve as reference groups. A similar argument might be made for "habitus," which in Bourdieusian theory (Bourdieu 1977, 1984) generates a personal sense of self and way of being. However, with few exceptions, scholars have failed to examine the processes through which habitus develops. Despite the scope of the Bourdieusian approach, the group and the responses of others are often missing. Local sociology depends on socially embedded self-conceptions, both those that emerge from one's self reflected in group involvement and those from the group having a collective identity.

To understand identity solidification, we not only focus on the individual as shaped by the demographic realities of public placement (race, gender, age, religion, nationality), but also recognize how identification emerges from the structure of social relations.

Identity develops as individuals recognize how others respond to them in those communal contexts that constitute their lifeworld (reflective identity), and through the recognition that, in choosing to participate in various groups, their decision reveals a shared selfhood (collective identity). Demography and sociality inevitably intersect. The force of this connection is felt in the group spaces to which demographic realities are tethered (Menchik 2019).

Reflective Identity

References to the "looking-glass self" endure because it is a powerful and convincing metaphor. We cannot know who we are until we realize how others respond to us. In the case of reflective identity, we see ourselves from the outside in. Social comparison theory (Pettigrew 1967) is a salient reminder that we only judge ourselves within an evaluative domain. One's self is judged in light of surroundings, drawing on the meaning of those spaces and scenes in which one participates (Tajfel 1982). In this way, the concept of reflective identity integrates structure, personal agency, and local context. It shifts Identity Theory from an impossible choice between "demanding" institutions and "mere" personal preference. Of course, to emphasize local context, we must consider the reality that most people participate in numerous interactional arenas. As we discuss, this permits the existence of mutable (Zurcher 1977) and plural (Lahire 2011) selves, or even more complexly hybrid selves. If we embrace the idea of a looking-glass (reflective) self (Cooley 1964 [1902]; Ruiz-Junco and Brossard 2019), it is because we belong to looking-glass communities that judge themselves through the responses of other communities.

Cooley's approach is particularly valuable in that it addresses how the self develops. The assumption – and it is a reasonable one – is that one learns to recognize the self as an organizing principle. That mysterious, not material, "thing" becomes known through gauging the reactions of others – at first ambiguous, later clearer. Throughout childhood, this reflective sense of self and its surrounding public identity develops. Cooley points to the moment of early childhood development of identity prior to the recognition of established communities. Children "see" their reflective self before they "see" their relevant public. However, even in one's first years, the realization of relations within the family – in whatever family form (Powell et al. 2010) – makes a looking-glass self possible. The presence of others, coupled with the desire to meet the expectations of those others, makes identity possible.

In time, identities, while mutable, become solidified, as individuals have a toolbox of selves from which to choose. Ultimately, some dimensions of potential selfhood gain higher salience and are used for ordering which are considered most frequently (Stryker 1980; Stryker and Serpe 1994). This approach operates within the symbolic interaction tradition, but, because of the formal categories of personhood, it is spoken of as structural symbolic interaction. Prioritized categories dominate how individuals think of and describe their selves.

This line of research, also known in social psychology as "Identity Theory" (Stryker and Burke 2000), frequently relies on experimental methods, and suggests that identity boundaries create selves based both on social categories and on group participation (Hogg et al. 2004). The argument is that identity is never simply about "me," but about "we" (Burke and Stets 2009). Of course, as noted, these "we"s do not necessarily refer to organized groups but may reference social categories, larger social segments, or even imagined communities. Although local sociology emphasizes that identities emerge from participation in and affiliation with groups, we do not claim that all identities are linked to this form of engagement. We acknowledge the value of these other, related approaches, even as we underline the importance of groups and reflective identity.

We also stress that identities are rarely simple depictions. Often they are multidimensional and evolve. This complexity has typically been ignored, particularly as a consequence of methodological limitations in experimental and survey research. As a result, identity does not completely map onto group membership (Turner et al. 1987). Nevertheless, while there are multiple templates from which persons draw and that oscillate in salience, the recognition of one's most significant relations shapes one's reflective identity. This is especially true when considering tight-knit communities, such as families, work teams, sororities, military units, congregations, and friendship cliques. Beyond these relations, as they are named, recognized, and defined, the places in which one is active build identity. Who one is becomes linked to the reputations of places in which one is routinely found. For instance, research on identity authenticity in workplaces, creating a "true" self, demonstrates the centrality of place as a means of self-definition (Sloan 2007).

Much work in Identity Theory treats the group as an anchoring point for the self, an argument made explicit in Manfred Kuhn's Twenty Statements Test (Kuhn and McPartland 1954). In this body of research, respondents were asked to answer the simple, if challenging, question, "Who am I?," over and over. While, perhaps, the questioning led to priming responses, the answers demonstrated that local communities with which individuals identified and in which they participated were crucial to identity claims.

In Kuhn's time, the answer to the question "Who am I?" might have been, "I am a Mason, I belong to the local Baptist church, I am a member of the PTA, I am a member of my family." While not every answer was so specific, many did refer to points of group engagement. Subsequently, reference group theory and social comparison theory, as developed in the 1960s, extended these claims, arguing that identity is tied to one's imagined affiliations. Individuals search for groups in which they feel comfortable and whose members they perceive as comparable to themselves, in order to reflect and evaluate their own accomplishments. Once this judgment is made and found useful, group standards become a model of identity (Dutton and Dukerich 1991).

Sociologists have been wary of using personal case studies, with their inherent anecdotal quality, but, perhaps ironically, individual case studies – psychiatric or grounded in autobiography (Bertaux 1981) – also reveal the complexity of reflective identity. For example, social psychology students reading *The Autobiography of Malcolm X* (Haley 1964) might find that his journey from being a self-described "hick" to a "hipster," a "hustler," a "prisoner," and eventually a "minister" and a "civil-rights leader" involved, in part, a journey through distinct local communities that shaped his corresponding names and nicknames: "Malcolm Little," "Detroit Red," "Satan," "Malcolm X," and "El-Hajj Malik El-Shabbaz." Which ones constituted the true identity of Malcolm Little? Did his identity – and our identities – have a solid core, many overlapping layers, or separate segments? In answering such questions, social psychologists have used multiple metaphors, some arguing that the self is like an avocado, others that it is an onion – still others, an orange. As local sociologists, we recognize the pleasure of these images, imagining a self salad.

Collective Identity

Although the metaphor of a looking-glass self is vital for understanding how one's identity is shaped by the reactions of others, this is not the entirety of identity construction. "Who am I?" becomes the equally significant question, "Who are we?" (Brekhus 2020). In the case of a reflective identity, embracing the judgment of others is crucial, whereas in the case of collective identity, what is essential is a community. Yet both forms of identity involve being shaped by groups.

Collective identities are often linked to groups or communities that individuals see as important, be they lived or imagined. Personal identities can be transformed into collective ones, but these are not necessarily the same thing, nor are collective identities merely the aggregate of individual ones. Instead, they involve the recognition of a shared status or relation (Polletta and Jasper 2001: 285, 298). Put another way, a collective identity assumes *both* a solidified group culture *and* a recognized interaction order. This poses questions as to the proper referent of identity (Brubaker and Cooper 2000). As Riley and Burke (1995) argue, a shared meaning structure develops among group members. Once this happens, collective memory can evolve. In other words, it is not just that collective identity entails participation in communal life, it also involves the willingness to treat shared history and culture as personally defining.

A meso-level approach to identity starts with a sense of being that is revealed through social embeddedness. In this way, one embraces a group self. Put differently, identity is built on the imagined legitimacy of one's presence as reflected in the eyes of others. Collective identity not only depends on interaction, but assumes that self arises from a belief that one is the type of person that properly belongs in the community, and that others will recognize that. Groups have *entativity* (Campbell 1958) – they are distinct entities – whose members have a common fate, routine circuits of action, shared goals, and interdependence. Collective engagement creates a belief that one can characterize oneself as a particular type of person, both personally and, crucially, to others. Of course, when judged from the outside, this can lead to privilege or discrimination, but it is how individuals come to have a stable feeling of who they are, what morality they share, and why their community is important (Greene 2013).

We define ourselves in light of the groups with which we identify, and by which others identify us. This claim is supported by Social Identity Theory, which, similar to Identity Theory, as described above, uses experimental research to show that identity derives from group commitments and boundaries, and, once created, they shape intergroup relations (Tajfel et al. 1971; Turner et al. 1987; Hogg, Terry, and White 1995). In turn, collective identity becomes the basis of actions from which we collaborate with others who have a similar perspective.

The belief that we share values permits us to accept perceived differences that otherwise might be disruptive. Cooperation is not inevitable, but a skill to which people must be socialized (Sennett 2012: 263). When communal selfhood generates the desire for social relations, help given and received is treated as essential and natural. As we aid others in our community – as is the case with farmers helping each other during harvesting or barn raising – we do so based on a firm belief, grounded in identity, that these neighbors properly belong to our world. Douglas Harper (2001), examining mutual aid in the North Country of New York State, describes this informal trading of labor as constituting a "neighborhood system." Help is given because of a consciousness of collective identity. Morale, so central to group success, relies on the willingness to cooperate because of an imagined commonality, despite potential differences.

As these examples show, belonging to groups shapes not only self-image, but action. The creation of collective identity has been treated as one of the fundamental challenges that social movements face (Melucci 1989). Groups expand through their ability to recruit and then socialize (Levine and Moreland 1994). In domains in which social problems are salient, the constructed identity and the value of agentic action are crucial to the continuation of participation in protest movements (Klandermans 1997).

Operating from Social Identity Theory, De Weerd and Klandermans (1999) detail this construction process in recounting how groups of Dutch farmers created identities in their opposition to both national and European Union regulations. Their economic conditions and their form of work caused them to think of their interests in opposition to the demands of EU bureaucrats in Brussels. However, the identification was not with all farmers in the EU, or even in the Netherlands, but rather with those in their specific region. Constraints on their choices challenged their expertise as farmers, and those with the most intense identification were the ones who were most likely to engage in protest activities. These challenges to the farmers' identity and competence placed them in a position that caused a rethinking of previously taken-for-granted selves. Farmers who might not have been politically active were now motivated to define themselves in opposition to what they considered oppressive demands; this forced them to consider how their freedom was limited by those who stood above them and over whom they had no control, and that in turn compelled them to resist.

While underlining the importance of collective identity, we do not wish to overstate its importance. One might join a group but then view participation as peripheral. Commitment is not automatic. Nor do we assume that a single master identity magically eliminates all others. Just as one does not participate in a single group, one may embrace other collective identities. Recent research and theory have emphasized that the idea of a single dominant self is inadequate and misleading. In line with the argument of Kenneth Gergen (1991), we can think of individuals as having saturated selves. Selves oscillate and become more or less salient in response to immediate circumstances, often treated as a feature of post-modernism. The French sociologist Bernard Lahire (2011: xv) spoke powerfully of the existence of "the plural actor," questioning the idea of the singular, stable self, emphasizing the effects of inter-actional contexts on the disposition to act. Still, whether one focuses on a dominant self or multiple competing selves, persuasive social psychological research traditions demonstrate that the local communities with which we feel allegiance shape self-definitions, revealing the importance of identity for local sociology and the value of a local approach for understanding identity.

Thinking in Cases

To appreciate how identity works in practice, we present data from a pair of ethnographic investigations. Although they do not express all of the intricacies of identity that are detailed in this chapter, they highlight the importance and the operation of both reflective and collective identities. The first involves observations of several cohorts of students who enrolled in three Master of Fine Arts (MFA) programs in the Chicago region to receive graduate degrees in the visual arts (Fine 2018). While the form of their art production varied widely, each student held to occupational goals that enrollment in graduate school helped them pursue, or so they believed. They entered with a set of inchoate artistic identities developed from their backgrounds and previous training. The programs shaped these artistic identities over their years in school. Three cohorts of students were observed and interviewed during two academic years. Observations focused on courses, class trips, parties, and informal discussions.

Central to the project was how aspiring artists fit into an academic community within the larger research university of which their program was a part. One program was located in an elite private university, the second on a large state university campus, and the third at a public university in a small city two hours from Chicago. Each cohort was small, with the programs enrolling 10 to 30 students at any one time. The focus was on the emerging identity of the students, rather than the faculty. The development of their individual and collective sense of being artists was crucial as they confronted an uncertain job market that would have to be negotiated after graduation.

The second project was an ethnography of students obtaining a Master of Public Affairs (MPA) degree (Hallett and Gougherty 2018). The examination of how these students came to see their degree and themselves as "professional" was based on two years of observations and interviews with students, professors, and administrators in the School of Public Affairs at what we label Central University, located in the Midwest. The Master of Public Affairs school at Central is recognized as one of the top such programs in the nation. The research consisted of following a cohort of students, observing their interactions with professors and with each other during required courses, popular electives, formal professional development seminars, and informal events ranging from hallway chit-chat to raucous parties. Interviews with students, faculty, and administrators allowed the researchers to question the implications of this occupational culture for the identity of these students who wanted to "do good" in the world, and to make a living while doing so. The research focused on the ambivalence that students felt as they developed a "professional" identity, and the tensions between the program's view of such an identity and their own view.

Becoming a Virtuous Artist

Art students enter graduate school with a set of production skills and a somewhat diffuse, if compelling, idea of what it means to be a contemporary artist, which they see as a virtuous self. Yet to become an artist requires a context in which an imagined professional role is ascribed meaning. Art school serves as that context. As in all forms of occupational socialization, this involves both the incorporation of judgments from others (forming a reflective identity) and embracing one's position in an occupational community (forming a collective identity). Both forms of identity depend on the community in which they are embedded.

The school is the site that fosters identity, through intense interaction routines and spaces of work. There are friends, rivals, a few frenemies, and numerous role models. Through the dialogue that is demanded in classes, the evaluations in which student work is publicly critiqued, and in informal gatherings, the idea of being an artist is shaped. As one student explained:

> Everyone responds to you as an artist. The expectation is that they take you seriously. That positive social pressure is one that would motivate you to keep moving, to keep making. It can be isolating to be an artist. If we don't have a supportive community and no one's pressuring you to be an artist, no one's regarding you as an artist, are you an artist?

In the context of these programs, everyone wants and hopes to claim an artistic selfhood, and then to find that selfhood validated by others.

For students in art school, the embrace of a collective identity might seem intuitively obvious. Students enrolled in MFA programs with some awareness of the occupational cloak they hoped to wear. Each had experiences in college, art academies, and even high school art classes that left them ripe for such identity construction. As they began their graduate training, many students desired to be specialists in particular genres – painting, sculpture, photography, or even conceptual art. These are identities that must be developed in contemporary art schools. Students started to develop a collective identity revealed by their affiliation with a community. But which identity? In these schools, genre labels were less important, and sometimes even pejorative. Painters, for example, must become "artists." As one faculty member explained to a group of new students, "If you're a painter, you're not just talking with painters. If you're a photographer, you are not just talking with photographers. That is part of the program."

By being embedded in this community and sharing an identity, narrow selves were extended. The artist can do more and, as a result, an identity as artist (or, more humorously, as a maker of "stuff") was embraced. One way that this happened is that the program emphasized that "anything" can be art and that they, as students, have the right to produce, discuss, and claim it. One faculty member laughed, "The joke about this program is that you can drag in a crushed can and we would critique it for an hour." The point was not about what can be art, but rather who they are as a community that they would be proud to treat a crushed can as an art project that deserves aesthetic respect.

The establishment of a larger "artist" category was jokingly revealed by the comment of one student. At one of the critiques of student work, Kevin, an admired student who "works with wood" (he creates sculptural objects that consist of pieces of wood nailed or glued together), was assessed with a tease from a faculty member, "You're kind of a wood guy. Maybe it's craft. That may be a bad word." Kevin vehemently rejected the craft label of "wood guy," while justifying his legitimacy as an artist, "People say why do you like wood so much? Nobody works with wood anymore. Then I say, 'I'm going to work with wood more. Fuck you.'" In an interview, he denied that he is

a "woodworker," a low-status identity, and insists that
wood is the material that he uses to participate in current
art world dialogues, just like paint or marble. Wood, with
its linkage to craft, became for Kevin a means of defining
himself as a transgressive artist, denying the *specific*
"wood guy" identity. Responding to the implication of
"only craft," Kevin wanted to erase the boundary with
craft and expand what a contemporary artist – a real artist
– can do, challenging the limits placed by those who might
police a strong boundary (Becker 1982).

What is clear in today's art schools, as well as in
galleries, is that there is a desire to create an identity
from a field that is characterized by malleability, rejection
of convention, and diverse forms of production. This
provides a challenge for establishing a collective identity
in that, given the variety of art practices, those who
participate in the art world must adopt a recognizable
sense of self.

To respond to this concern over occupational segmen-
tation, art students preferred to define themselves using
the generic title of "artist," rather than with a specialized
occupational label. Painters and photographers, with their
specialized equipment and occupational history, were
tempted to use those more specific titles. However, most
students felt that the identity label of artist served them
well, permitting an extended community. The entire
cohort – no matter the form of practice – served as their
community.

In this regard, one student explained that he didn't
define himself as a filmmaker, although his films were
admired; he felt that accepting this identity might suggest
that he belongs in film school, but this, in his view, was
not who he was. It violated the collective identity that he
embraced: "I feel like artist is a broad enough term and
describes an approach to doing things, so that I am not
limited by material. So [I am] just an artist who does a
variety of different things." Being in art school revealed
his identity. It was the basis of building a community

that transcended genre, while embracing an honored label.

A collective identity serves as a warm blanket, but art school also involves creating a personal identity. It is here that reflective identities emerge. Given academic politics, these claims are often as much about social categories as about the signature style evident in a body of work. Meaning is viewed through a demographic lens, for some artists leading to a marketable persona.

Take the case of Carlos, a Latinx student, who presented a performance – an artistic performance – in which he emoted loudly into a microphone with electronically generated feedback, creating a deliberately inarticulate language that in its raucous chaos was intended to reveal threats to his self. He described this as the politics of identification. Perhaps responding to his ethnicity, one faculty member asks, "Is this piece about the reclamation of some historical identity?" Similarly, but more contentiously, Michelle presented an "installation" of objects that referenced her Catholic upbringing and her struggles to be an artist with a religious sensibility. She referred to the importance of the "comfort of touch." Michelle's work was condemned by several faculty, with one rejecting the "lovey-dovey metaphor of social unification" and another, more sharply, describing the church as a genocidal institution, advising her to stop being this kind of artist if she hoped to succeed in a secular art world. These comments had effect. Michelle, near tears at the critique, explained later that she chose to emphasize other themes in her student career.

To be an artist – that is, to have an identity as an artist – is not a given. Or, perhaps put better, it is given by others who share a social world. One knows where one stands because of the responses of others to one's work and one's identity: not only to the artist as a person, but to seeing the artist through the lens of their projects – a tinted looking-glass. One is the kind of person who paints, draws, sculpts, films, or performs in a particular way.

Art does not speak for itself; it cannot, in isolation, produce a reflective identity. One requires the performance of artist-hood that comes from the offering of words and bodies along with objects and performances. One needs others to respond to one's presentation in a way that permits the community – and, crucially, the maker – to feel that the label applies (Helguera 2012: 11). Creating an artistic self depends on reflected judgments of others, just as does the creation of the work itself.

Being in groups is central to graduate student life, leading to relational linkages that matter deeply, establishing both collective and reflected identities. As one student admitted, contrasting university life outside her department with her intimates, "these are my people." Her colleagues hang together, debate, gripe, celebrate, and commiserate, and come to award meanings to selves. Their belief in a community, working together while separately, is crucial to any semblance of occupational identity. Everything counts in learning who one is, who one wants to be, and what really matters. In art school, students – proto-artists – create a local world that, before you can enter and be embraced, demands a performance of self. Identity thrives in such intense settings.

Becoming an Ambivalent Professional

The process of identity acquisition is not always seamless, but it is always linked to local cultures, whether informal or institutional. Although few would readily embrace a disliked identity, at times its benefits are accompanied by costs; participating in a desired social world may entail the acceptance of such costs. This is evident in the case of a Master of Public Affairs program. In the ethnography of an MPA program, "professional" is both a collective identity and a reflective one, a view sponsored by administrators and confronted by students. The program holds a mirror to the students. In many ways, the program *is* an active mirror, not just reflecting but projecting out to the student body and defining what is "professional" within the context of the group culture. Yet, as individuals and as members of their peer groups, the students also reflect this culture – admittedly, with much ambivalence.

The original focus of the project was to explore how aspiring managers learn the rationale of accountability as a technique for directing organizations (for instance, public schools). However, debates about professional identity were evident as faculty and administrators created a culture in which to embed their students. The first Dean of the program discussed the founding of the School of Public Affairs: "It seemed to me what the field really needed was a *professional* management program, and that's what I thought the school, this school, should be. And we structured it accordingly, so if you look at how we're structured fundamentally, a business school in the public sector in some ways – we never said that, but that's really what we were." He was clear that he intended to create a culture that was to shape identities, and these identities were to rely on the template of professionalism. Other faculty and administrators likewise used the symbolic designation of "professional" as a touchstone. A veteran professor explained that "the MPA is a professional terminal degree for people that want to go and do work in the public sector." This became a core element in the creation of the identity of students.

The students, however, did not arrive with a specific desire to be seen as "professionals." Their sense of what the institution could teach them was diffuse. They were not motivated by status concerns, but rather by a vague desire to benefit society. As one said succinctly, "I knew I wanted to do something to help people." Another remarked, "No one is here because they want to make a bagillion dollars." A classmate elaborated: "I think the sentiment underneath the whole thing is that people want to make a difference. And they're gravitating towards careers that may not make them as much money as they could, because they're all highly capable individuals, if they pursued other avenues. So money is not a measure

of success for these people, is my sense." Students were
looking for the community to translate these values into
forms of interaction and characteristics of selves.

Given the students' vague motivations, how, then, did
they learn a collective "professional" identity? Socialization
began early, during a week-long intensive "Mini-Math"
course held just before the start of classes. On the very first
day, the program director told the students, "Math is a
tool, an important tool" for what they would be doing "as
professionals ... analyzing ... interpreting ... managing."
Learning math was, in this sense, a moral enterprise. The
students were immediately taught that the school believed
that whatever they might do in their careers, they would
act as "professionals." At the end of Mini-Math and
heading into orientation week, the Director of Graduate
Student Services explained: "Monday is the start of your
professional career."

In the months that followed, the students embraced
this proffered collective identity. During an interview, a
student described the degree as "professional" because
of "the way you're taught to quantitatively look at quali-
tative issues, it teaches you a way of thinking. And that's
what a professional degree is, it's a discipline, a way
of approaching a problem and the tools to do it." Like
artists, they were taught locally in ways that reflected the
expectations of the larger occupational world.

Students accepted this collective identity both because
they could see the benefits and because it was expected
of them. Being professional implies status within their
desired social world. Although the students came to the
program with the goal of "doing good," and prestige
was secondary, they wanted jobs and careers. Embracing
this identity was a way of doing well, as well as doing
good. Nevertheless, as they considered their own reflected
identities within the community, they expressed cynicism
about the training they were receiving.

Students understood that they had to perform as professionals. Following the collective messaging of the program,

they came to accept that a professional identity involved a certain demeanor, or what was colloquially termed the "MMD," the "Masters of Managerial Deportment." This was a crucial – and, for some, a surprising – part of their training. Students needed to recognize an interaction order that had not been central to their pre-training imagination. As a result, demeanor was a concern of administrators who lamented that students lacked "polish." The administrators decried how, despite the program's high ranking and rigor, on the job market their students lost out to the "Kennedy Kids," referencing slick Harvard graduates.

The administration and faculty were earnest in emphasizing polish, but some students rejected this demeanor as a mere performance that suggested an inauthentic reflected identity. One explained, "I think it's fake. I think there's a lot of forced etiquette that goes into it, like, I feel like there's a lot of rules, you know. I don't want to ever feel like I can't say certain things or not be myself." This student added, "I feel like I don't ever want to be defined as a professional [Laughs]."

Other students were more pragmatic. As one explained, "I feel like it's very easy to not care about your appearance or how you look in class. I hate that appearance matters, but in the real world that's a huge factor." Although opinions varied, there were at least two problems with the "deportment" aspect of the professional identity being projected by the program. First, as a result of their placement, the students were not yet professionals, and perhaps their small-town, public university environment made this more of a challenge. Instead, they often embraced a student role (Becker, Geer, and Hughes 1968). Recognizing this contrast, one student joked, "You can be unprofessional while getting a professional degree!"

Second, MPA students drew a contrast between their local culture and that of the MBA students who occupied the building next door, sharing a library with the MPA program. Students satirized the MBAs for their formal clothing and "fake" deportment. One student scoffed at "their shiny shoes and business tans." Despite the similarities of the MBA and the MPA, these students rejected the perceived financial motivations of the MBA students and defined themselves as "not like them" and disdained the "polish" that this similarity implied. They didn't want shiny shoes or a tan, and they anticipated making less money while doing more meaningful work. Their local culture was powerful.

Despite the students' ambivalent responses to the collective identity projected by the program, what was most significant about their training was that they conceptualized their role as participants in a group and in an emerging occupation. The local context of the training, in a small Midwestern city, shaped these views. Their attitudes toward professionalism and deportment were not personal judgments – or at least not entirely – but were linked to the group culture of their program. Certainly, variation existed among these men and women. Some students were attracted to the academic substance but not to the desired deportment, enjoying their informal culture. Others imagined professional careers in elite spaces. Still, it was the MPA program as a local culture that shaped selves. Students could find a reflected identity from faculty and colleagues that allowed them to fashion a compatible self in light of images of their occupational market. In this, they could adopt a collective identity from their local cultures. These aspiring policy professionals relied on their local context to develop identities that they felt and hoped would serve them well. In this, despite their differences from emerging artists, in aspirations and paths into markets, the practices of identity work were strikingly similar.

Group Being

We argue in this chapter that understanding identity in light of a local sociology perspective depends on two processes: the transmission of reflective identity, and the embrace of collective identity. Both must be activated and motivated in a social context, but they operate in distinct ways. While identity is treated as highly personal, the personal is social. An identity is developed by recognizing the responses of others in a variety of contexts (reflective identity) and by recognizing that one's choices of participation reveal that one is a particular kind of person (collective identity). In both cases, the local establishment of identity is crucial. Identity markers are not given from afar or developed from within but are established from one's surroundings.

As we argue subsequently in discussing belonging and bonding within groups, who one is and what is important leads to commitment and the drawing of boundaries. While collective identities derive from inclusion, they also depend on exclusion. While much of our account is based on fieldwork, the examination of identity depends on the impressive experimental work that has developed Social Identity Theory as well as ethnographies of the development of occupational identities, as in our studies of becoming an artist and a policy professional.

None can deny that identity is a core building block that contributes to personal assurance and social order. Could a functioning modern society exist without citizens finding a realm of belonging for themselves? Confidence and order can only occur because of small communities to which people become tightly tethered, and that become a crucial part of their routines. As a result, we begin with an understanding of the person in the world, but it is a world that is, at first, highly differentiated. Self begins with family, friends, classmates, fellow congregants, teammates, and co-workers. They judge us and we desire to claim a mantle that covers all within the scene. In time, members of these groups are seen as part of larger categories, such as race, ethnicity, gender, age cohort, political perspective, or religion. However, whichever broad category is invoked, identity construction begins with sociality. Identity can never stand apart from its originating group context.

Ultimately, the sense of being that emerges from social relations is what situates the individual within a local world. These ties develop from how actors are responded to and how the group impresses itself upon them. This is the heart of sociality, stemming from a belief that identity is always given: through reflected judgments and by collective cultures.

− 3 −

Belonging to Groups:
The Power and Benefits
of Commitment

Sane people did what their neighbours did, so that if any lunatics were at large, one might know and avoid them.

George Eliot, *Middlemarch*

While people participate in groups for many reasons, why do they *remain*? The answer, we argue, is that they develop a feeling of belonging and, as a result, the group matters to them. Groups do more than coddle selves and cobble identities; they also contribute to participants' satisfaction and their enjoyment of the achievement of desired goals. They supply friendship and offer the pleasures of co-presence. As a result, local sociology depends on an understanding of the feelings that being a part of a group inspire. As we have learned from the disorienting, dismaying isolation caused by responses to the COVID-19 virus, humans crave contact. Social distancing has its costs.

In this chapter, we describe how friendship generates belonging through commitment and social capital. Believing that one belongs to a community produces the confidence that allows people to feel engaged with others as they come to share a worldview. Admittedly, people may participate for other reasons – for example, financial need in the case of a work team. However, unhappy members often feel that "I don't belong." How do groups generate communal relations and how do these connections matter? Recognition of "Being in Groups" is the first component of a local sociology; "Belonging to Groups" is a necessary next step.

Belonging: Friendship and Commitment

Local sociology holds that groups and societies, in order to flourish, require a powerful "culture of friendship." This stance recognizes the significance of mutual engagement, empathic concern, and shared affect. However, we expand the idea of friendship from merely the positive relationship between two individuals. Instead, we aim for an analysis of friendships that emphasizes the affirmative role of affiliation and tight-knit networks. These social clusters connect the individual to the wider world. Network analysts who study webs of attachment (Laumann 1973) have long promoted this claim. As a result, our focus on the power of belonging and commitment does not emphasize dyadic ties, as important as they are, but groups that are characterized by allegiance, support, and consensus. As these connections are associated with the resources and the placement of participants, social capital is integral. To be sure, intimate ties and the security that they bring often inspire personal creativity, but the friendship group and the affiliative network generate communal creativity based on the embrace of local communities of trust. To understand how community builds society, we must invite "friendship back in" (Kaplan 2018).

Friendships have the potential to provide a foundation for the *good society*: a quilting of trust, creating a secure safety net for civic engagement (Bellah et al. 1991: 116). In trusting our friends, we become committed to participating in circuits of action that justify seeing oneself within a larger world that stretches beyond one's colleagues. These domains – imagined, and yet powerfully real – include the nation, the citizenry, and ethnic groups. They acquire particular meanings and shape our activity through group affiliations. In this way, the group is a model for a larger community, making identification plausible and comforting. The ability to talk with others provides the basis through which community life develops political capacity (Honohan 2001; Allen 2004).

Both the ideology and the practice of belonging permit social systems to be based on what Ferdinand Toennies (1887) speaks of as *Gemeinschaft* relations, in contrast to *Gesellschaft* structures. This is the divide between community and society. Put another way, society is only possible because of caring communities. Although caring communities today depend on the resources that other communities provide (the Durkheimian division of labor), local worlds are – at least in the ideal – worlds of trust.

In proclaiming the importance of groups, belonging, and friendship, we do not wish to overstate our case. People leave groups, and ties can be disposable (Desmond 2012). Despite the romance of friendship, social relations are not necessarily characterized by equality, harmony, and durability. Even if affiliative ties are desirable in principle, they also have the potential in practice to divide and to reflect privilege. By definition, friendship is marked by exclusivity (Polletta 2002: 4). These concerns that link closeness and exclusion must not be ignored. Even saints have resentments, and even bigots have chums. In fact, bigots require comrades to prevent them from being isolated because of their otherwise deviant and rejected beliefs. Moreover, the 1% can rely on their resources and stature to make alliances with the 99% that can undercut a more equal and genuinely diverse society, as when the rich patronizingly treat their help like family but keep their wages low, or when a White person exclaims, desiring a believed sincerity, "I have Black friends." As Jo Freeman (1972–3) argues, friendship ties among elites – coupled with an absence of transparency – support control from the top. Bundles of friends, despite often burning brightly, can cool and darken. Groups can set themselves apart from others. The existence of sets of intimates does not presume a single cohesive community and may, in fact, make it less likely.

It is easy to recognize how friendships promote preferential treatment. Friendships can, and do, create a world that is gendered and racially hierarchical. For example, many worry about interlocks among those who serve on corporate boards, as many members are male, White, and Ivied. At present, eight of the nine Supreme Court justices, despite their diverse politics, have Harvard and Yale degrees. The power elite may be becoming more diverse (Zweigenhaft and Domhoff 2006), but it is still an exclusionary club. While we should not dismiss the Aristotelian belief in the virtues of friendship and the possibility of cross-boundary connections, we must not erase the vices of preferential statuses.

Nevertheless, while friendships can generate inequality, they also provide opportunities for advancement (Cherng, Calarco, and Kao 2013). In theorizing how social ties knit society, Mark Granovetter (1973) demonstrates that both strong and weak ties allow for engagement, although in distinct ways. Weak ties permit people to span interactional gaps, creating a more diffuse and dispersed network, while strong ties establish confidence in immediate support that allows for a warm and comforting sense of place. Each is important, and recognizing this accords with the "relational turn" in social theory (Crossley 2011; Donati 2011; Donati and Archer 2015). Groups are always relational sites.

To the extent that we can claim that friendships stabilize community, *sociability* becomes a central element in group affiliation. This challenges the Simmelian view that informal interaction lacks a concrete instrumental purpose (Simmel 1950), embracing instead the perspective of Erving Goffman that it is through interaction that commitment is generated, and, as a consequence, those who have an extended network benefit. Although friendships emerge from dyads, dyads build on each other, creating structures of affection, as in cliques or clubs. However, more than this, friendship nodes permit social and even political belonging. Hannah Arendt phrased it well in suggesting, "Friendship is so eminent a republican virtue." In her view, successful statecraft depends on a politics of friendship. Arendt asserted that friends are "partners in a common world – that they together constitute a community" (Gebhardt 2008: 335–6). Friendships do not necessarily produce a recognition of shared fate; however, when that perception emerges, we witness the power of close ties.

The Benefits of Belonging: Social Capital and the Citizenry

It is precisely because friendships are important that scholars examine friendship trends in contemporary society. Concerned, some suggest that the average number of close friends that an individual claims has declined, along with an increase of those without intimate confidants (McPherson, Smith-Lovin, and Brashears 2006). While this claim has been challenged, Eric Klinenberg (2012) points out that there is an increasing tendency for people to choose to live alone. Even as the implications of such findings continue to be debated, the COVID-19 pandemic has underlined the costs of separation from friends.

Concerns about individual isolation and the attention that these findings create may distract from the fundamental importance of *groups* as sites of friendship. People commonly remain in groups because of the feeling of belonging that friendship brings. Yet, as important as togetherness may be, the skeptical reader may ask, how do acquaintanceships affect society? The answers, we argue, can be found in the multiple benefits of belonging, especially through social capital in civil society.

By elevating friendship to a central place in local sociology, we draw on the work of scholars who argue that social ties provide crucial support for those who cope with personal challenges (Pescosolido 1992; Perry and Pescosolido 2015; McCabe 2016). We need not overcome our dilemmas alone. Sociologist of religion Robert Wuthnow (1994) finds that such ties characterize Americans, but political scientist Robert Putnam (2000) fears that these crucial relations are in decline, risking not only personal welfare but perhaps the whole of civil society. Putnam laments the decreasing membership and organizational fragility of once robust formal associations that, in a bygone era, dotted the landscape. In contrast, Wuthnow (1998) argues that informal small groups often have filled the void. Wuthnow's optimism tempers Putnam's alarm, yet both argue compellingly for the benefits of the ties that are built through friendships.

Friendship, and the commitment to sociability that flows from ties that drip with emotion, constitutes a resource for purposeful action. Following Wuthnow, Putnam, and many others, we label this "social capital" (Bourdieu 1986; Coleman 1990; Portes 1998). As a form of capital, these relations are valuable, both in their own right and in the pursuit of desired ends, whether individual or collective. Although the instrumental term "social capital" does not always reveal the positive emotions that we think of as being crucial to friendship, it presumes the existence of supportive acquaintanceships. Such relations are transactional as well as emotional: a favor bank. However, social capital is not simply the number of friends one has or the number of groups in which one participates. What is crucial is that these established relationships allow us to make legitimate claims on others (Lichterman 2005), whether for a ride to the airport, a couch to surf, a reading of a manuscript, a loan, or something bigger.

Groups, whether they spring from an informal setting such as a neighborhood garden or more formal settings such as religious institutions, are incubators for social capital. The resources that these ties entail can be vast and deployed in diverse group circumstances: from those in wealthy suburbs to those in inner-city barrios (Small 2004). These relations also create opportunities for leadership. They boost solidarity and efficacy, increasing confidence in participating in a variety of domains, including politics and social activism (Keohane 2014). The idea that one is part of a team with resources and emotional support motivates people to engage in what otherwise might be considered contentious activity. Robert Putnam's (1995: 167) definition of civic engagement, "trust, norms, and networks that can improve the efficiency of society by facilitating coordinated action," underlines the connection between social capital and the development of local communities.

Commitment grows with the recognition of a community of support that generates attachments, trust, and emotional affiliation (Burke and Stets 1999; Brint 2001; Stets and Cast 2007; Lawler, Thye, and Yoon 2009). Through interaction, one becomes aware of the skills, resources, and networks of others. This recognition allows for the development of social capital, establishing mechanisms for transforming interpersonal relations into desirable outcomes, through material resources and useful infor-mation. While civil society can be interpreted as a network of meaningful relationships, it operates through the mutual engagement of the participants, whose actions depend upon their *recognition* of the reality of the relationship. Network associates not only provide information, they also motivate colleagues to engage with a group and to advance shared interests. The local is expanded, even into the public sphere.

Through intersecting groups, social capital builds expansive networks, creating the possibility of organiz-ational recruitment via who one knows and how one

knows them. As David Snow and his colleagues described
for the Nichiren Shoshu Buddhist movement, a school of
Buddhism originating in Japan, American adherents joined
through networks, building on their established relations
(Snow, Zurcher, and Ekland-Olson 1980). Individuals
are embedded in multiple networks with crosscutting
linkages, and this increases the amount and breadth of
recruitment into social movements (McAdam and Paulsen
1993: 640).

Only later, and while building upon a foundation
of ties, do mass media bolster personal recruitment.
Movements thrive with close-knit supporters, even if
they have only occasional linkages with groups of greater
power, substantial resources, or institutional centrality.
The social capital of participants potentially generates
commitment to costly action (Della Porta 1988), which
has the potential for overcoming the collective action
problem in which potential members assume that they can
stand back, letting others do the heavy lifting of activism
(Olson 1965). For example, Marc Sageman (2008) speaks
of a leaderless jihad in the post-9/11 era, arguing that
terrorism consists of "informal local groups . . . conceiving
and executing from the bottom up." Who needs Bin Laden
in a world of Facebook and hookah bars? Any clique
can become a violent cell if there is a sufficient desire to
belong that can then justify attacks. Of course, not only
terrorist cells are at issue. Partisan bands that begin as no
larger than a small group, but in which commitment is
strong, provoke revolutions and insurrections. We see this
today with groups on both the left and the right that use
a potent and distinctive group culture and the willingness
to bear costs to commit participants to actions that few
others might accept. As the storming of the Capitol or the
demonstrations after the death of George Floyd vividly
illustrate, these groups rely upon the presence of common
convictions, have the ability to move swiftly, and motivate
adherents to trade the comforts of apathy for the risks of
engagement.

Dramatic examples aside, it is an open question as to whether the decline of civic groups, such as the PTA or bowling leagues, reveals declining interest in civic participation. If this is the case, what is its cause and what is its effect? While Facebook and online groups may have (in part) replaced suburban Parent Teacher Associations, Robert Putnam's implications in *Bowling Alone* are that society depends on an *ecology* of groups that support forms of social capital that undergird a healthy civil sphere.

Included in the benefits of belonging are a sense of control and belief in the ability to shape the social surround. Here we point again to the neighborhood effects literature in which researchers of urban poverty find that a sense of collective efficacy predicts positive community characteristics. A neighborhood is a bounded spatial domain in which friendships emerge through propinquity (Festinger, Schachter, and Back 1950). The contextual and ecological features of a local urban interaction order are essential for analyzing the organization of inequality (Quillian and Pager 2001; Sampson, Morenoff, and Gannon-Rowley 2002). Robert Sampson and his colleagues argue that large structural forces are mediated by neighborhood groups with their distinctive cultures, linked to local institutions that encourage or retard the development of collective action and social control. Put simply, collective efficacy – a belief that those in the neighborhood have the power to generate change – develops from local conditions (Sampson and Raudenbush 1999; Sampson, Morenoff, and Earls 1999).

Although social capital provides a compelling image of the value of friendship, any metaphor that monetizes sociality is not without challenge. Nor should it be. Is it the individual who benefits from social ties? Is friendship a thing that is owned by a person, or is it characteristic of certain forms of sociability, dependent on shared expectations? We argue that it is the latter. Groups constitute network nodes that extend beyond the social ties of any actor. What is achieved is a sense of togetherness, even when members are physically apart. Moreover, it is not simply comradeship that matters, but the existence of group places – physical or virtual – in which that comradeship can occur. Further, beliefs about the propriety of social relations arise from judgments about what kinds of people belong together, encouraging certain friendships and discouraging others. The forms of commitment that develop are not merely an outcome of communal politics – rather, they build those politics as they provide opportunities for communication, shared projects, or the assignment of stigma.

This is not to say that commitment lacks costs: some social ties, with their temporal demands, constrain participation in other activities. Relations can be greedy, preventing those involved from extending their network or sharing activities. As Lewis Coser (1974) explained, marriage can be a greedy institution in this sense, limiting outside engagements. So, too, is work in a world of workaholics. To suggest that social ties inevitably create broad commitments neglects exclusive friendships. Personal relations within local cultures must be consistent with identity in order to create new affiliations, and these changes depend on circumstance. Nevertheless, to the extent that those within an interaction order see themselves – like the farmers in chapter 2 – as having common goals and challenges, the ability to draw on social capital increases.

In many ways, churches (and mosques and synagogues) illustrate the benefits of belonging and have proven to be powerful examples of the potential of tiny publics (Djupe and Gilbert 2009; Tavory 2016). Churches are no panacea, but the desire for comradeship, coupled with a recognition of shared faith, pastoral leadership, an identifiable group culture, and a space in which members jointly participate, make many church communities models of how local organizations produce a powerful collective consciousness.

As Lim and Putnam (2010) demonstrate in their analysis of the effects of belonging to church congregations, these groups, while ostensibly reaffirming faith, generate a web of social relations that support a community of believers, fellow congregants, and their institutional leaders. In addition, the schedule of services and the comforting solidity of houses of worship provide a time and space in which admired others are likely to be found. Joining a congregation – no matter which deity is worshipped – increases life satisfaction, by not only producing confidence in the afterlife, but creating comfort in this one. Articles of faith matter less than the coffee served after the sermon.

Congregations provide social services and the satisfactions of fellowship (Wuthnow 1994; Chaves 2009). In claiming the salvation of souls, they create conditions in which salvation through the care of one's neighbors is possible. This perspective suggests that the specific beliefs of the denomination are not critical if congregants feel a tight commitment to each other's welfare. Souls are saved within a beloved community in which culture is created through collective worship.

Despite this heavenly view, congregations vary in their values, structure, resources, and preferred modes of discourse (Bartkowski 2000). It is easier for a church to provide support for needy members than to provide support for those equally needy outside the congregation. This is one reason that liberal churches, particularly those in wealthy communities, are less likely to display the tight communion of those in economically challenged locales. Liberal churches are rarely the central institution for their parishioners, who often have other groups to which to turn. Psychiatrists are prioritized over priests. In contrast, the communal ideology of conservative churches is more demanding of commitment and may reflect the greater needs of those who join.

Not all congregations generate positive affect, as conflict over resources, beliefs, or personnel can strain harmony within church communities (Becker 1999). Nevertheless, commitment to other seekers is often as powerful – or more so – than one's relationship with the divine. While faith-based groups are an exemplary form of community, leisure worlds – such as reading groups or sports teams – also demonstrate that shared culture can create social capital if a common purpose builds a caring community (Long 2003; Amenta 2007). Although social capital is embedded in personal relations, group ties that depend on individuals linked in a shared space are an especially powerful means of generating networked resources.

Part of the power of voluntary groups is that, through selective recruitment, relations are based upon homophily – the similarity of participants as judged by their demographic characteristics, habitus, past cultures, and present preferences. This similarity makes the process of commitment easier to achieve on the local level (McPherson and Smith-Lovin 1987). It is not simply an ideology of togetherness, but the outcome of an interaction regime. Even if a group includes individuals with diverse backgrounds, the reality that they are collectively engaged can lead to a blossoming of unlikely friendships. The act of belonging and its recognition provide participants with tools that encourage them to see their commitments as crucial. The security that engagement provides creates confidence in one's identity, a local community, and the larger structures that can seem distant without a firm belief that one belongs.

Thinking in Cases

To illustrate the dynamics of belonging, we rely on two of Fine's ethnographic projects: studies of restaurant kitchens, and of high school debate teams. In the book *Kitchens: The Culture of Restaurant Work*, Fine (1996) observed four restaurant kitchens in the Twin Cities for a month each. He watched in the kitchen, occasionally helping with minor tasks. In addition, in each restaurant he interviewed most of the backstage staff.

The restaurants selected represented the upper end of dining in the area, with one an elite gourmet restaurant; the second, a high-end continental restaurant; the third, a local steakhouse; and the last, a hotel kitchen. During lunch or dinner, the cooks prepared meals as ordered by their customers, and the hotel restaurant also served banquet food. In each, a tight-knit kitchen community existed, and, from this, dishes were created that were judged to reach a superior level of aesthetic and sensory proficiency in light of the standards and the niche of the restaurant and the desires of diners. Employees did not necessarily admire or trust all of their colleagues, but they recognized that they shared a world in which all were invested. Given the gendered composition of the community of chefs and cooks at the time, they could be described as a "band of brothers."

The second project, *Gifted Tongues: High School Debate and Adolescent Culture* (Fine 2001), examined a distinctly different research site, suburban public high schools in Minnesota. This research focused on the dynamics of two high school debate squads over the course of a school year. Several dozen students engaged in competitive policy debate, an extracurricular activity held at weekend tournaments in which each two-person team debated a proposition for a year. In some rounds, the team took the affirmative position (in the year studied, the topic was prison reform), and in other rounds they took the negative, attempting to defeat the plan of their opponents. A judge, often the coach for another school, decided the contest. Fine attended classes, extracurricular meetings, and local, regional, and national tournaments.

To be an effective debater, one needs skills in addition to being articulate and a good researcher. What is important is that participants consider themselves part of a team that shares ideas, research, and strategies. They distinguish themselves from those whom they are competing against, and also from those within their school who are outside of the group. Belonging to the debate squad is a means by which adolescents find a home turf in what might otherwise be an impersonal school environment. Despite their differences, what connects the two studies is the salience of belonging. This extends identity as described in chapter 2 to a connection with a group. Being part of a kitchen crew and a debate team not only established identity but promoted a desire to participate in both the group culture and required tasks. This can occur in the context of employment or leisure, but a sociologist of the local knows that in both cases the group matters, even if these colleagues were not originally chosen as friends. In time, given their shared activity, time together, and common spaces, friendships are likely to form. These friends can be counted on for support. Being a part of the community generates commitment to the work at hand.

The Commonwealth of Cuisine

In examining kitchen culture, we can speak of the commonwealth of cuisine. In most cases, and even where there is conflict between employees and managers or among employees, successful workplaces are sites of belonging: a world in which people care about each other – people know your name, your abilities, and your background. They watch you work and watch your back. Of course, to care is not inevitably positive – one may be watched with thorny eyes, and stabbing in the back is hardly unknown. Kitchens are deeply social spaces, an intensity shaped through steam, sweat, speed, hierarchy, and the hazards of knives and fire. This is kitchen confidential. Restaurants are typically minute associations, given the limited number of employees and focused tasks. Kitchens are places of talk as well as action, and they are sites of social capital to be utilized for career advancement and job mobility.

Considering a workplace as communal treats belonging as creating a link between an interactional perspective and an organizational sphere: a micro–macro linkage.

The occupational culture tethers staff to the workplace. However, this is not only a matter for the identities of the individuals involved – belonging provides the organization with tensile strength. Thus, we find in numerous groups – including restaurants – a persuasive metaphor that the organization is a primary group. One cook noted of his experience, "I like the closeness that you have in the kitchen. I love people in kitchens . . . It's like a family. You can tell each other exactly what you think. It's like all your brothers and sisters." Some informants even suggested that the head chef is like a father. Whether the kitchen is seen as "one big happy family" or as a dysfunctional one, that metaphor is powerful.

Of course, there is a danger of manipulation by authorities in treating the metaphor as real. This was particularly apparent in the hotel restaurant, where many workers felt alienated from management. "Family" can easily become inauthentic. As one cook explained: "When Bernice [a pantry worker] started, [the chef] came up to me and said that I want you to go up to Bernice and say, 'I'm glad that you're working [here].' Like I'm a personnel director. I looked at him and said, 'Are you serious?' and he said yes. 'Now,' I said, 'wait, I'm not going to do that.' How cornball." Belonging must emerge organically in the context of a legitimate interaction order and group culture. When trust and affiliation do not result from ongoing social relations, it leads to skeptical or sarcastic remarks where the emotional context of affiliation is absent. In this case, the chef lacked the social capital to make this request, even though he had the authority to direct the staff in culinary tasks.

In the best case, the diverse backgrounds of those in the kitchen lead to trust, personal warmth, and the willingness to accept being a global workforce. In their interviews, cooks explained that they enjoyed the "international cast of characters," reflecting the racial and ethnic diversity that characterize urban restaurants (and especially the kitchen backstage) as workplaces. These connections provide social and economic opportunities that stem from group relations. Cooks often arrived before the start of their shift and remained afterwards to help co-workers. In addition, they sometimes chose to "hang out" to talk with friends, receiving a free lunch or libations from the bar. One cook even organized a "Booze Cruise" for friends.

From local affiliations, a career can be built. The hospitality industry has traditionally had substantial mobility. One can quit a job and rapidly find another. However, and perhaps ironically, the high rate of turnover among restaurant staff indicates that one can belong to the occupational community and not a particular place. A result of this industry churn is the networks that affiliation provides. Friends point to new employment options. As Mark Granovetter (1974; see Prus and Irini 1980) noted, acquaintances (or, in his terms, weak ties) provide job market opportunities. This was clear in the case of Barbara, whose husband was acquainted with the owner of the restaurant for which she was eventually hired. Brandon, the owner, suggested that cooking might be the right occupation for her, and, with his encouragement, she enrolled in a culinary trade school. She was eventually hired part-time to make desserts, and soon was promoted to pastry chef. She came to belong.

This affiliation matters in structuring life chances. A hotel cook told a similar story about a waitress:

> She was getting new furniture, and I was moving at the time, and she said, "Do you want some chairs?" and I said, "Sure." . . . She said, "Well, I know somebody who's looking for a cook," and so she called up the guy, and he came over with a twelve-pack of beer, and we sat there and got drunk, and he said he'd hire me.

Perhaps her convivial willingness to chug brew helped, but her network provided social capital. Another example reveals how previous employment affected future employment: "I talked to the chef [at a previous job], who was a friend of mine. I told him I wanted to leave . . . So, he said he'd talk to Tim, because Howie used to work there before. . . . And he thought maybe he could bring me over here. So, he talked to Tim [the chef]." In the interviews, these connections, shaping job mobility, continued throughout their careers, from dishwashers to head chefs.

Arguing with Culture

The world of high school debate has a very different contour, yet belonging is equally important. It is generally true that high school students do not move from school to school, and, as a result, this world lacks the fluid mobility networks of restaurant kitchens. Still, during their high school careers, established debaters come to know teammates and opponents. They develop caring concern for those on their debate team and those in the debate world. We can speak of high school debate as composed of group cultures, but also of a local and a national subculture. For many students negotiating a large and, for some, alienating high school, a debate squad provides a place to be. With similarly positioned classmates, they find social capital and friends within the school setting. The team provides a safe harbor within the hectic whirl of high school life, demanding a temporal commitment and a social investment.

These features lead to relationship work and a collective sense of being. In all cases, the students desired to belong. While the relationship with one's debate partner was often primary, having some of the intensity of being in a marriage or working in a patrol car, the feeling of belonging to the larger group is crucial as well. As was clear through the observations, the relationships that developed provided benefits outside the walls of the debate classroom, offering opportunities to find romantic partners and participate in the drama, politics, and pleasures of high school life.

For adolescents, commitment is filtered through the demands and encouragements of parents, and these demands must be negotiated. Consider Darrin, a high school junior, who hoped to be more involved with the team, but whose parents did not see debate as having priority for the family. Once, Darrin called his parents to ask if he could go with several teammates to the local university library for research. His parents insisted that he had to babysit for his siblings. The coach was disappointed because she hoped Darrin would become more integrated into the team; she even joked that she would babysit in his place. The same coach described an instance the previous year of a female student who went on an unapproved date and whose parents grounded her. The coach complained that these students had committed to the team and that parents should not punish them by undercutting their obligations and responsibilities.

For the core members of the squad, their affiliation was primary; the hope was that the virus of commitment would spread. One assistant coach, while a senior in high school, lived with the family of a fellow debater when her parents moved out of state. This was taken as a noble act that demonstrated her devotion. The fact that many high schools, including those studied, set aside a room for the debaters to which they could retreat after school cemented this loyalty: this was a messy but safe space for these teens to hang out.

The temporal commitments that teams require can be extensive. Some debaters – labeled "debate bums" – spent extensive time doing research for competition, neglecting class assignments. In extreme cases, these fanatics received academic probation. One former team member explained, "I debated and went to high school on the side." Another said, "I spent a whole year working harder than ever. I mean that's all I did. I spent all of Christmas break working in the library. So, I killed myself and then I graduated." This caused problems for these teens as the intensity of their belonging could interfere with other domains. They were seen as having "no social life," and often they resented those less deeply enmeshed in the team culture. While intimately engaged, they could be criticized as having walled themselves off from those features that constitute a balanced teen life. The issue for a tiny public – a group that hopes to have impact on others – is to adjust the level of commitment so as not to overwhelm, but to incorporate. This is true in many spaces, but it is dramatically evident in arenas in which participation is voluntary and the exit cost is low.

Group Belonging

In this chapter, we describe the virtues and dilemmas of belonging. Belonging depends on venerating social relations, a central feature of local sociology. Tight engagement creates conditions for coordination to achieve shared goals, relying on social capital to permit those who are a part of the group to gain new opportunities. In extending the local sociology perspective from analyzing identity as a connector of self and others, belonging focuses on the continuity of social relations.

Friends run in packs, monitoring those in other packs. Caring communities depend upon this. The commitment is to a relational place, a choice of action, and, most significantly, a set of others. This reality gives network connections special weight within a larger, more expansive, and more consequential society. However, this only happens when people believe that, given who they are and what they do, they belong together. The space they share is more than simply a stage for action; they are an acting troupe. Each performer depends on every other member of the company. Our two cases, though very different in content, are spaces in which belonging is crucial. Whether performing for each other, for other workers in the scene, for hidden customers, or for a set of seemingly impartial judges, action is evaluated and becomes meaningful in building and cementing relations.

These profound ties provide a context that supports group continuity. First comes identity work that is linked to a recognition that one's self is integrated in a group. This, then, promotes a deeper feeling of belonging. Belonging generates actions that publicly demonstrate commitment, and this level of commitment allows for group stability that promotes further involvement. As a consequence, the effects of belonging to a group are cyclical. This recognition of the intersection of group life and affiliation reveals the power of the local in creating a solidified society.

– PART II –
THE WORLD OF THE GROUP

− 4 −

Building Groups: The Power of Idioculture

We write these words now, many miles distant from the spot at which, year after year, we met on that day, a merry and joyous circle. Many of the hearts that throbbed so gaily then, have ceased to beat; many of the looks that shone so brightly then, have ceased to glow; the hands we grasped, have grown cold; the eyes we sought, have hid their lustre in the grave; and yet the old house, the room, the merry voices and smiling faces, the jest, the laugh, the most minute and trivial circumstances connected with those happy meetings, crowd upon our mind at each recurrence of the season, as if the last assemblage had been but yesterday!

Charles Dickens, *The Pickwick Papers*

The power of Dickens' writing is apparent in how it resonates with the reader, who easily recalls how seemingly "minute and trivial circumstances" create connections and assemblages that stay with us and shape how we act not simply in the moment, but in the *durée* of time. Dickens' compelling words and rich insight engage deeper questions for sociologists, and for local sociology more specifically:

What channels group activity in ongoing interactions? The answer, as we argue in this chapter, is culture, leading to a host of additional questions: What is culture, how does it work, and where does it reside? Our perspective, grounded in social psychology, asserts that the locus of culture is found not only in society-level entities or in individual preferences, but most importantly in joint experience, in social worlds, and in communication networks: the very connections and assemblages of which Dickens wrote.

From the standpoint of local sociology, culture is a form of practice that joins shared understandings with social relations. As "practice," it consists of meanings that are crafted and used, actions that are performed and viewed, and objects that are manufactured and consumed. These practices are crucial in building groups in two senses: first, in providing the content on which groups are built; and, second, in forming or shaping ongoing interactions.

In presenting the localist approach to culture, we draw from classic works that, although once eclipsed by the structural dominance in sociology, are again coming into vogue. August Hollingshead (1939: 816), a prominent scholar of community life and author of the book *Elmtown's Youth*, suggested that "Persons in more or less continuous association evolve behavior traits and cultural mechanisms which are unique to the group and differ in some way from those of other groups and from the larger socio-cultural complex. That is, every continuing social group develops a variant culture and a body of social relations peculiar and common to its members." In order to build a group, some elements of the *culturescape* must be salient (repeated often) and central (impacting group structure). However, not every element of a group's interaction enters its idioculture, and, further, not every element of its idioculture shapes structure or increases commitment.

Despite Hollingshead's insights, for sociologists culture has more typically been linked to the large-scale social systems that characterize expansive populations (described as macro-cultures or, sometimes, treated as national cultures), or has been connected to individual preferences and personal experiences (described as micro-cultures). In distinction to both of these perspectives, we focus on the meso-level which can connect the two approaches, treating groups as cultural systems. We argue that meaning emerges from the middle, incorporated by institutions and embraced by persons. Interacting groups and tightly networked populations are cemented through shared understandings and the routines that constitute circuits of action. This hinge leads us to recognize that a key locus of culture is found in joint experience, in social worlds, and in communication networks.

This local approach has several virtues. First, it specifies the content and boundaries of cultures. Second, it permits a comparative analysis of groups. Third, it recognizes that groups are cultural units. Finally, it demonstrates that cultures mediate environment and action.

From "Big" to Local: The Character and Content of Culture

On occasion, social scientists, as well as the wider public, refer to those aspects that they claim reveal national cultures: American culture, French culture, or Brazilian culture. These analyses provide perspectives that display how societies differ, suggesting that each society is "exceptional" in its own way and differentiating a people or a nation from others. However, because of the diversity of any sizable population, an analysis that presumes the existence of a national culture is necessarily imprecise, even if, like James Joyce, we conceive of a nation as consisting of the same people living in the same place. In practice, national culture is splintered, even if citizens imagine that they are united. Dublin is not Limerick or Belfast, Catholics are not Protestants or Buddhists, and the affluent are not the stevedores. In its totality, a national culture is often conceived as everywhere and nowhere, sensed but invisible, and never quite definable.

While nations and regions reveal aspects of a shared character that is evident in their collective representations, the goal from the perspective of local sociology is to determine how these beliefs and values have effects through the presence of an interaction order. Beyond this, we explore how multiple group cultures – similar to each other in the characteristics of their members, networks, or common milieu – create *claims* of togetherness, given institutional support through media representations, commemorations, memorials, and state edicts. People believe that larger systems are meaningful, but what matters for local sociology is how and to what extent these meanings are made manifest in ongoing interactions.

While cultural sociology must do more to examine these interactions, one of the main traditions in social psychology largely ignores culture. Experimental research typically treats groups as content-free, even though histories and traditions allow participants to recognize community. Despite connections with institutions or societies, culture is acquired and used in local domains. In laboratory studies, groups are often treated as interchangeable. Given the difficulties of operationalizing cultural content in lab studies, groups are rarely assumed to be *meaningful*, but it is through common meanings that commitment is built.

Local cultures can generate intense affiliation and build sturdy boundaries, conveying symbolic messages about implicit norms (Bjorklund 1985). Every interaction order depends on a set of references that historicize the group (Mechling 2001), a homegrown style that filters and situates collective representations. In establishing a history, shared references build cohesion (McFeat 1974; Eliasoph and Lichterman 2003; Ignatow 2004). This continuity encourages the organization of face-to-face gatherings. Interaction builds shared knowledge, and shared knowledge builds interaction (Carley 1991). As a result, interaction and culture are mutually implicated in establishing social order, making shared experiences local, anchoring identities through the perspectives of meaningful others.

The linkage of action and history is evident both in experimental studies of cultural transmission (Rose and Felton 1955; MacNeil and Sherif 1976) and in ethnographic studies of group life (Sherif and Sherif 1964; Wiley 1991). Groups are crucibles in which culture emerges, relying on decision-making strategies (Harrington 2008), traditions (Collins 2004), shared ethos (Patrick 2006), or negotiated practices (Hallett 2003). Solidified group knowledge creates boundaries, separating insiders from those who stand outside the realm of understanding. Collaborative circles are the sites of activity, identification, and friendship (Farrell 2001). Groups support a shared vision, but simultaneously they are fragile as personal trajectories may veer in various directions as participants find other worlds to join, or discover that what once was compelling has become unsatisfactory.

Sociologists are not the only ones who speak of the power of local worlds; management theorists also promote the value of a strong organizational culture (Ouchi and Wilkins 1985) and warn of the risks of intraorganizational hostility (Weeks 2003). Despite wishful thinking, culture is not always a balm. As Joanne Martin (1992) emphasizes, competing idiocultures within organizations potentially divide and antagonize. As we describe in chapter 6, countercultures may compete with those that are integrative.

The collective meaning systems that we label "idiocultures" separate group action from untethered interaction that lacks affiliation and history. Informal cultures also are distinguished from the training within large organizations in which socialization and affiliation are more highly structured. Meaning derives not from an interaction order as such, but through *continuing* interaction. This leads to the recognition of boundaries as crucial to establishing the group as a meaningful and desired place (Cravalho 1996).

Ultimately, cultural choices become communal through action, a recognition that privileges performance: the doing of meaning, not just the learning of it. To understand how groups are built, treating culture as action is crucial. This is found from primary groups (such as families) to secondary groups (including clubs, churches, or cliques) to networked segments that are linked together through routine communication, spatial co-presence, or choices of consumption.

Groups and Their Idiocultures

Every interaction scene, no matter how minute, mundane, or mutable, establishes a set of self-referential meanings. These bits of communal understanding are built from the opening moments of group life and, in time, are shaped by what Craig Rawlings (2020) terms "cognitive authorities" – those group members that others look to in developing group beliefs, norms, and practices. As we describe later in this chapter, Fine wrote of the organizing role of group culture and the role of leaders in determining what cultural forms are appropriate for groups to endorse. The original ethnographic data were from over four decades ago in his three-year examination of Little League baseball teams (Fine 1979). Likewise, Rawlings finds group-motivated changes in attitudes among intentional communities as well. This recognition of the power of group dynamics in shaping attitudes and action has been applied to a range of other social domains, such as mental health organizations, summer camp cabins, congregations, workplaces, and social movements. Group cultures are present in every ongoing interaction scene, and they provide stability that aids in the persistence of group life.

While the recognition of ongoing interaction and the continuity of social relations are important, what gives these features stability is that the relations and the interaction are *about* something. Content matters. Some group cultures – for example, those of policy makers (Janis 1972; Gibson 2012) and bureaucratic organizations (Herzfeld

1993) – have more resources, authority, and, as a result, more external influence than others. However, all group cultures develop local norms and shared preferences. We find accounts of strong group cultures in numerous sites, including Israeli military units (Sion and Ben-Ari 2005), Middle Eastern terrorist cells (Sageman 2008), Argentinian opera lovers (Benzecry 2011), and Japanese motorcycle ("bosozuku") tribes (Sato 1991): a global range. Wherever participants find continued interaction, cultures are built. This meso-sociological approach, attending to the conditions that generate shared meaning, asserts that the establishment of traditions, shared references, and customs is integral to group potency. As Lawler, Thye, and Yoon (2009) have argued, different group structures produce distinctive "micro social orders," although, as we have shown, these features of social life are better described as "meso" because they cannot be reduced to the simple acts of individuals.

We argue that any sociological understanding of group cultures must recognize the extensive institutional influences that direct local scenes, channeling shared action. The backgrounds of participants, coupled with their expectations, expand a group's meaning system when a salient occurrence sparks recognition of collective experience. These triggering events incorporate external cultural themes within local discourse and action. Once established, cultural elements become a cohesive force whereby members recognize the value of their group. Communal cultures build on background knowledge (the known culture), the moral standards of discourse (the usable culture), the instrumental goals that facilitate action (the functional culture), and the claims that support the recognized status hierarchy (the appropriate culture). What eventually characterizes group life results from immediate interactional demands (triggering events, as noted above).

In the following pages, we illustrate this process through research on Little League baseball teams and fantasy gaming groups, but first we briefly describe each component. The known culture consists of the prior knowledge and past experiences that can be retrieved and activated for inclusion in the meaningscape. Members often have a wide cultural awareness from being part of multiple groups. This serves as a pool of background knowledge from which participants can draw in creating their culture.

The usable culture includes cultural elements available for interaction. Some topics cannot be shared or said in public spaces. The definitions of such "taboo" or "politically incorrect" things vary across groups, but some things are deemed illegitimate as part of general discourse. Groups differ, of course, on what is publicly legitimate, and talk can be shared privately. Some locales are *obscenity factories*, sites in which cursing and profane language are accepted and acceptable. The restaurant kitchens discussed in the previous chapter are such venues; additional ones include political backrooms, police stations, gang turf, military barracks, and the like. In other sites, faculty meetings or church picnics, for instance, such talk would be inappropriate or might even lead to sanctions. Many modes of propriety exist, but all groups have some form of usable – and, therefore, unusable – culture.

Successful cultures must be more than acceptable. They must also permit the group to solve problems that might otherwise prevent desired goals from being achieved. We term this functional culture, not in light of macro-structural functional theory, but in the pragmatist sense that these cultural elements permit the group to operate more effectively. Cultural formations are a form of collective problem solving (Becker and Geer 1960; Spector 1973). Every group with common aspirations and desired outcomes must determine how to accomplish them through the promotion of shared practices, as when weather forecasters speak of the dangers of what they term yo-yoing forecasts, in which a worker, newly on shift, immediately changes the forecast of the meteorologist who was replaced.

The fourth component, the appropriate culture, emphasizes that status hierarchies structure acceptable meanings. Not everyone has equal status, recognized by both participants and scholars. While the promotion of certain cultural traditions might articulate a change in reputation, idiocultures typically reflect and support the interpersonal network and power relations. Local cultures develop in ways that are consistent with the social positions of members, a process that we find in high school debate clubs in which team leaders have their jokes become part of club lore and their rules become the ones that novices must follow.

Finally, we speak of triggering events as those actions that spark talk or further actions. Once triggered, these potential memes enter into an ongoing group culture and may become a point of reference. Freudian slips, for example, prove to be a rich vein of nicknames and anecdotes. These triggers serve as what Neil Smelser (1962) described as a precipitating factor for collective action. Operating in tandem, these five factors permit participants to build their connections through a solidified and bounded culture.

The advantage of a group-based approach is in its ability to understand how participants create culture through an interaction order that depends on the recognition of shared pasts and planned futures. Meaning is always contextualized and cannot be divorced from actors or action.

Group culture reflects collective memory, current needs, and future dreams. Once traditions are established, groups unite around them and defend them, a means of establishing cohesion and trust. This emphasis is evident in research on *collaborative circles* in the arts and politics (Farrell 2001), leisure domains (Corte 2013), and scientific groups (Parker and Hackett 2012). These studies reveal the stages by which groups are built and how they may dissipate. Tight-knit circles create culture, and this culture supports these tight-knit circles (as well as occasionally disrupting them, described in chapter 6). For example, as Andrew Perrin (2005) clarifies, civic organizations depend on local dialogues that take varying forms depending on the organization's values and focus of activity. Religious communities engage in distinctly different forms of discourse compared to leisure or political ones.

Idiocultures solidify small groups in all institutional realms. The local culture provides a cognitive and emotional structure through which individuals build collective pasts and plan for shared futures (Katovich and Couch 1992). Inevitably, these cultures have a temporal dimension. By recognizing their common perspectives, participants invoke these traditions with the expectation that others will appreciate their meaning. Group cohesion depends on shared comprehension.

A local sociology must also recognize that some traditions are closely held, hidden from those outside the community. The classic cases are the secret society, the criminal gang, and the fraternal lodge. Awareness of culture reflects what members may treat as the private, even sacred, quality of the group, capable of betrayal. Indeed, some societies, gangs, or lodges maintain severe sanctions for revealing internal matters. To share this information with outsiders is felt to diminish the intensity of ties within. This is particularly true when the information that is disclosed threatens the desired public face of the group. Consequently, groups become notably less open while in public spaces in the presence of what are often termed "civilians," metaphorically linking the group to a military outfit. This caution also applies to new members who may be shielded from the contentious beliefs until they demonstrate that they can be trusted. Full acceptance occurs gradually as the novice has mastered significant portions of the culture that is available and has acted in accord with group demands, often passing a behavioral test.

Local Sociology and the Building of Groups

Idiocultures not only supply the content on which groups are built, they also provide the environment that directs activities, much in the way that stairways, hallways, and elevators direct traffic. That is, idiocultures channel continuing interaction. Here we draw from Jeffrey Goldfarb and his evocative image of the sociology of small things. This potent imagery captures the *place* of action. Goldfarb uses an exceptionally small place – the kitchen table – as a basis of analysis. His point is not simply that small, mundane cultures are valuable, but that the environment under which they are produced allows for the construction of allegiance through the shared understandings that arise. By building a tight-knit culture, these domains support and direct joint actions. The salience of presence – being in the same physical locale – provides for both social relations and the development of shared meaning.

Through his research in Eastern Europe, Goldfarb (2006: 15) uses these "small things" to describe the development of social relations and cultural content that are built despite the yoke of repressive governments. He writes that "When friends and relatives met in their kitchens, they presented themselves to each other so as to define the situation in terms of an independent frame rather than that of officialdom." Flowing from the hearth, friends and family establish a framework of meaning that permits the group to recognize that they have agency, despite sanctions from above. Community members recognize that their participation in shared spaces contributes to affiliation. Such an analysis applies to a wide range of repressive regimes, both in the Global South and in the Global North.

The self-referential meanings that communities develop allow for the establishment of collective knowledge. As a spatial marker of group life, the hearth becomes a central symbol in the resistance to Eastern European authoritarianism, but the crucial point is that kitchens and porches are found everywhere. They are meeting points through which primary relations are strengthened and discourse reacts to challenges from those with more power. Hearths help to establish a remembered and referential past. Other places of discussion, central to a robust public sphere, include bookstores, salons, and clubs, as well as open meetings and gatherings (Habermas 1989; Mische and White 1998: 706; Emirbayer and Sheller 1999: 732). In these close places, participants assume that others share a sense of being and belonging (Gieryn and Oberlin 2015). Small cultures shape the public interest, support an energetic social system and civil society, and, as such, can be described as "tiny," but vital, publics (Fine 2012).

By viewing culture from the meso-level, a local sociology addresses several salient challenges. A robust culture demonstrates how innovation, socialization, affiliation, and change are manifested in action that, when successful, builds a strengthened group. Treating a cherished place as the central crucible of social stability situates culture at the critical junction of the individual and the institution. In this way, groups reveal cohesion and disaffiliation, smoothness and disruption. Even if participants do not always see themselves contributing to a collective project, they may respond to the projects of others by relying on the bonding that connects them with those others, as we describe in chapter 5.

For those who wish to orchestrate an idioculture, be they leaders, coaches, or directors, the challenge is to organize unpredictable, unscripted interactions, taming them through a set of beliefs concerning how the group "ought" to operate. This requires keeping interaction flowing and social relations in play. The problem is that events that shape collective life are readily understandable after the fact (reading backwards) but cannot be determined before they occur (looking forwards). As a result, the construction of a meaningful culture is neither automatic nor easy. Participants must align ongoing, unpredictable behaviors with the established interaction order, unless they deliberately choose to disrupt those assumptions. Even if people cannot predict the moments of everyday life – the jokes, insults, errors, or queries embedded in conversation – they nonetheless treat the interaction order as something that must remain salient for predictability to exist.

Despite their fluidity and continual adjustment, conversations and collective action become routinized, grounded in shared practices, and embedded as circuits of action. Conversation analysis emphasizes this point, finding formal structures at the most granular level of talk (Schegloff 2007). This suggests the relative stability of the group over time and space. Even when action sequences are altered, participants persuade themselves that they remain much the same, evolving incrementally. Even as change laps at the edge of the social, the idea of constancy is essential in permitting interaction rules to be treated as valuable. Despite the solidification of lines of action, breaks in coordination and questioning of culture serve valid social purposes, such as persuading participants to consider the moral basis of their actions. Either smooth or rough interaction can build meaning, as long as the former does not create passivity and the latter avoids long-term ruptures.

In building a culture, groups can cement their history through a commitment to ritual. As Randall Collins (2004) emphasizes in his work on "interaction ritual chains," interactions have larger implications when connected to other interactions, chains that are the basis for macro structures. Commitment to interactions inserts the importance of recognized occasions into what otherwise might be free-floating group life. This analytic focus replaces fleeting, untethered social situations – what have been termed "ephemeral micropublics" or "Goffman publics" (White 1995; Ikegami 2000: 997) – with those that recognize the continuation of meanings and a firm group character. As a result, our view stands apart from the fluidity that one sometimes finds in accounts of the interaction order. In contrast to a perspective that treats behavior as a response only to the actions that have immediately preceded it – seeing interaction as a form of continuous adjustments to an ever-changing and unpredictable stage, what Charles Tilly (1996) memorably refers to as the "invisible elbow" – localism emphasizes a stable group life through norms, standards, and expectations.

With this stability, *practices* (actions understood by reference to local cultures) are central in that participants connect their shared activity to a recognizable spatial or relational domain, such as the kitchen table that Goldfarb depicts or the ordering of batting practices among Little League baseball teams. Actions within those places in which social ties are displayed constitute a grounded performance. If this is not precisely scripted, the synopsis of the play is evident. The stage depends on actors and audiences that are aware – admittedly imperfectly – of what is expected of them.

Treating these groups as tiny publics suggests that every ongoing group constitutes a local outpost of society. Even if actions extend beyond the interacting group, the boundary, as recognized by participants, consecrates the actions within and clarifies who belongs and who must stand outside. The local scene both mirrors and distorts the larger culture, with its style, rules, and beliefs determining how social relations should be transacted.

Thinking in Cases

In this section, we examine how group culture builds community within two ethnographic domains: the worlds of Little League baseball and fantasy role-play gaming. These were early ethnographic projects of Fine (1983, 1987) and were conducted at the point that he was arguing for the importance of idiocultures in structuring group life.

The first project, *With the Boys: Little League Baseball and Preadolescent Culture*, involved a three-year study of ten Little League baseball teams in five leagues located in suburbs of Boston, Providence, and Minneapolis–St. Paul. Fine spent his spring sitting in the dugout, hanging out with the boys before and after games, and occasionally driving them for ice cream. He asked questions of both players and coaches, focusing on the team, rather than parents. Drawing on laboratory studies, the questions included: How are small groups organized "in the wild"? And how does culture emerge within the context of the group *in situ*? In this regard, Little League baseball teams – comprised of approximately 15 preadolescents (mostly, but not always, boys) – proved to be productive sites in that these teams had both the drive to win (an instrumental goal) and a desire to have fun (an expressive goal). Meeting two or three days a week for several months in the spring, the players on each team, in collaboration with their coaches, developed customs, nicknames, and jokes.

By the end of the project, it was clear that, although the research site was fruitful, the culture that developed was limited. Boys met for several hours and most of the time was devoted to playing baseball, a structured activity that did not permit much in the way of discussion. What would a more intense culture look like? The second project, *Shared Fantasy: Role-Playing Games as Social Worlds*, conducted over 18 months, examined world-building. Groups of tabletop fantasy role-play gamers, those who played *Dungeons & Dragons* and similar games, proved to be such a community. These games were played in the community room of a local police station and in the homes of players. Most of the participants were young men, typically between 15 and 25 years of age, many with a deep knowledge of medieval lore, science fiction, and fantasy novels. The participants hoped to create a vibrant imaginary world, and often the activity lasted from early evening until late at night and into the early morning hours. Like Little League teams, each group had a distinctive interpersonal culture, but within the game world, they also created a broader fantasy culture, not so different from the little communes that contemporary gamers today create online in games such as *Minecraft*.

Culture on the Diamond

Little League baseball teams provide a window into how local cultures are built. Even though teams continue from season to season, they typically have half or more of their players "graduate," aging out of Little League when they turn 13. In addition, not having played as a team for the past nine months and comprised of 15 young athletes who attend a half-dozen local elementary schools, they must develop a new culture each year, shaped by those coaches who continue.

By examining Little League teams throughout a relatively brief season, it became possible to observe the development of distinctive team cultures. At the inception of any group, a culture does not exist, but the awareness of shared meanings begins from the opening moments of interaction. When individuals meet, they begin to construct a culture by asking for names and other biographical information for later reference (Davis 1973). These early pieces of information – first impressions – often have great weight in typifying players. Such beginnings become the basis of what comes later. Names lead to nicknames, and backgrounds often lead to jokes. On a Minnesota team, learning that one player had recently moved from Chicago, his teammates referred to him as "Deep Dish" after the regional pizza style. Meanings imported from outside (the background culture) provided a cultural template. In time, idioculture became self-generating as the experiences that the players shared provided material from which local cultures were built. Eventually, shared experiences became the basis of team life and provided the basis of supporting or undermining the adult authorities.

From the first practice, a solidified culture is built. A player who joins after that first meeting must learn the established norms and practices in order to be treated as a full member. This is a challenge of joining a group already in progress, a feature that those who are newly married often face in dealing with in-laws. As team culture develops, it becomes a basis for references and action. Some boys who join a team during the middle of a season are never fully accepted, a phenomenon found in schools as well. In this way, laughing at the jokes that others make, telling jokes at which others laugh, and sharing gossip are important.

In observing Little League baseball teams, it became evident that these seemingly mundane moments were crucial. One boy quit his Little League team only 10 days after he had joined. Part of the problem was that he never learned enough of the local traditions and gossip to be considered a teammate; as an outsider, he was shunned. To belong means to know and express the idioculture of the group. However, not all seemingly mundane moments become part of the idioculture. Incorporation depends on the processes of idiocultural development that we described earlier: these elements must be known, usable, functional, appropriate, and triggered.

As noted, the first criterion for whether a potential element enters the culture of a team is whether it is part of the background information – the known culture – that the players can access. Teams rely on their stock of latent knowledge (Becker and Geer 1960). Even though group culture emerges from interaction, what is said and done is anchored in what is previously known.

Consider the reference to a "Polish home run" in one league in suburban Minneapolis. The expression would be meaningless absent a supportive context. Beyond the mundane suggestion of a home run, there exists a symbolic opposition of drilling a pitch over the outfield fence and popping a foul ball straight over the backstop behind home plate. In either direction, players spoke of a "home run." However, this phrase required knowledge of stereo-types. During the research in the 1970s, "Polish" was an

ethnic slur that implied "backwards" or "incompetent."
Absent this background, the identification of such a foul
ball would not be possible. Creativity poses no problem
for a recognition of background culture, in that it represents novel combinations of previously familiar elements
(Hebb 1974). The mixture is awarded a different meaning
from its components. Innovations, seemingly idiosyncratic, derive from previous knowledge, as long as the new
formulations make sense within the interaction order.

The second criterion for affiliation is that the cultural
element must be usable; this varies from group to group and
from situation to situation. Can players avoid punishment
when saying or acting out these things in public? Consider
one team in which a star player objected to a teammate
speaking of the "fucking umps." Another player objected
to the epithet "Jesus Christ," taking the Lord's name in
vain. On other teams with different standards of decorum,
these remarks would not have sparked an objection. The
presence of coaches, particularly middle-aged fathers,
was often sufficient to limit what these preadolescents felt
comfortable sharing publicly.

The third element is whether the tradition helps to
achieve team goals, either instrumental or expressive. This
constitutes the "functional culture" of the group. The rules
and restrictions that players impose are felt to improve
performance. One team enforced a rule that they would
take batting practice in the order that players arrived. As
batting practice was a desired activity, the rule encouraged
promptness, and, on occasion, the entire team arrived at
the field before any of their opponents. Players set this
rule, not the coach, and it strengthened the position of the
leader who lived close by.

To be fully accepted, team culture must support the
status structure. A tradition that denigrates a leader will not
succeed. This is clear when it comes to nicknames, which
are often evaluative. During the first year observing one
team, older teammates gave Tom Mayne, an 11-year-old
substitute outfielder, the nickname "Maniac," reflecting

both his last name and his awkwardness. This revealed his low status. The next year, he started at third base and was one of the best batters. Team members forgot – or chose not to use – his previous nickname, and his new nickname, "Main Eye," indicated his higher status. These are not the only cultural elements shaped by status. Jokes and pranks are as well. Who sponsors a tradition matters in light of the power of esteem. On one team, an admired player got a short haircut, called a "wiffle." Because of his sponsorship, many players followed, but such buzz cuts were not common elsewhere.

Finally, we find triggering events. Some event provides a spark that creates a comment or action that enters local collective memory. Successes solidify rituals, and taboos result from failures. Players on one team called their coach's old automobile a "Cadillac" after a foul ball almost hit the rusty car, and he jokingly warned the boys not to hit his Cadillac. The wayward ball and the coach's joshing sparked a catchphrase that continued throughout the season. In contrast, the coach on another team provided his players wristbands, worn to express solidarity. However, after they lost their first game, these accessories were never seen again. They provoked the wrong memory.

These five components work in tandem. We provide an example that incorporates each. During the middle of the season, one team established and enforced a rule that players could not eat ice cream while sitting on the bench during a game. A combination of events triggered this rule. It started during a game in which the team, by then accustomed to victory, was behind. One of the nonplaying, low-status players was casually licking an ice cream cone while seated on the bench. Seeing this, the high-status players ruled that, although gum could be chewed, ice cream was not permitted. The rule was known to be compatible with how professional players comported themselves. It did not violate taboos and was consistent with rules that children are permitted. Further, it was functional in relieving the frustration of older players during the game and in directing the attention of the younger players to the field. Finally, it was appropriate in that higher-status players proposed it to control those with less status. The rule stuck.

Fantasy Cultures

The world of fantasy role-play gamers reveals a different density of cultural production than found in the comparatively limited engagements of Little League baseball. While the same processes exist (known, usable, functional, appropriate culture, and triggering mechanisms), they operate in a more expansive context. Role-playing games create what Alfred Schutz (1967) spoke of as a "universe of discourse." Their imaginary worlds powerfully craft a complex lamination of everyday life. More significantly, the culture that gamers share, along with their psychic investment in their characters and their collective desire for the gaming party success, entails an intense group life.

Unlike competitive games, role-playing games, such as *Dungeons & Dragons*, are structured as cooperative scenes. The competition, if we can define it as such, poses the players against challenges that the Dungeon Master has set for them. Within the group, there should be no loser. As a result, a powerful culture establishes a commitment to sociality. However, as we pointed out with regard to Little League baseball teams, a status hierarchy exists that the emergent actions must heed.

Given the dual level on which role-play games exist, one observes the culture of the characters in the game and in the culture of the players. Both levels generate meaning, and they are integrated. They generate affiliation even after the game is complete. We focus on these two levels in describing a group of young men who met for six or seven hours each week. The imagined culture of the characters affects the players' friendship culture and vice versa.

The development of any friendship culture mirrors the form of other friendship groups, as detailed above. In one group, Howard, a taxi-driver in his mid-twenties, was the most skilled referee, but he was also a lovably irascible person. Each week he would bring a basket of peanuts that he refused to share. One week, Fine brought a large bag of potato chips that Howard almost completely devoured. When he left the table, Fine ate some of his peanuts, although no one else dared. As one player jokingly warned, Howard "knows each of his peanuts." Howard's peanuts were central to group lore, but also structured the group through the power of social control. On another occasion, a player came to the game wearing a T-shirt bearing the word "Buttercup," and, as he was a low-status, peripheral member, the name stuck.

This is similar to the cultures of Little League teams. However, these players were also collaborating in developing a world that involved those imaginary figures that they role-played. The friends around the table shared a culture, but so did their imagined characters. While not psychiatric, this constituted a collective fantasy: a legitimated *folie à deux*. Through performance, meaning is generated. This is not so different from the actors in the television sitcoms *Friends*, *Cheers*, or *The Office* having a culture as professional thespians and their characters having a culture within the scriptwriters' world, but for the gamers it goes still further as they lack scripts and are simultaneously creators and actors.

Meanings in the game world evolve from the experiences of the gamers *and* of the characters. As a result, the characters *as characters* can meaningfully refer to the game events, a point emphasized by Erving Goffman (1974) in *Frame Analysis*. While imaginary characters do not recall events, their animators do. This becomes more vivid as games continue from week to week, or even month to month. We can think of the gaming party as having a collective memory. As one player commented, "I think our group can relate to past games . . . about their characters, and then, if someone joins them, he wouldn't know what's going on." Players repeatedly recalled a previous evening in which the party of 5 humans and 1 dragon had to fight 1,000 orcs, surviving only because of the dungeon master's recognition of the dragon's power. On another occasion, in a science fiction-based universe, participants regularly "remembered" the "disaster" caused by a spaceship breaking through the dome that covered a city on an airless asteroid, killing all residents.

Particularly striking is when fantasy culture integrates natural friendships and character connections. This connects a player's behavior to an event in the game, or a game event to real-world relations. Each frame can comment on the other as part of group culture. While most games are based on medieval imagery, groups laminate that history with contemporary interpretations. These young men enjoy sharing parody spells, permissible through the looseness of game boundaries. Instead of the feared black magic spell, Finger of Death, players speak of the comic spell Finger of Hiccups. Characters, supposedly medieval, may be treated in a similar jocular fashion. One preteen had been acting in a silly fashion, making distracting jokes. Finally, an older player, whose character was a mage, announced, "I turn him into a piece of bread. I may toast him." For the next several minutes, the group treated him as if his character had been turned into a slice of bread. This became a continuing theme. Three months later, when another young player talked too much, a group member noted, "Remember when we turned that kid into a piece of Wonder Bread?"

Idiocultural transformations can also be keyed from reality to fantasy. Natural interaction can be transformed within a pseudo-medieval universe. One player related a humorous story about two gamers who went on a date. According to his account, nothing went right. They could not get theater tickets and the man's car broke down. When his friend learned this, he laughed, "My spell worked." On another occasion, when a player's dog began to bark, its owner remarked, "It's Dandy in his lycanthrope [wolf-like] phase." These examples suggest that the line between frames of meaning can be breached in shared discourse. Little Leaguers and fantasy gamers both have rich cultures, but for the gamers the culture has an additional layer. The group, seemingly one, contains two distinct meaning frameworks: two cultures around a single table.

Building Groups

While the culture concept in sociology has often been linked to macro-sociological analysis, culture as a form of meaning-making, routine, and negotiated order belongs to the meso-level as well. We must look to groups to understand what is at stake. This is the beating heart of local sociology. Culture is ultimately comprised of meanings that are crafted and used, actions that are performed and viewed, and objects that are manufactured and consumed. These are necessary to build the group, extending a sense of being and a belief in belonging in a way that makes the engagement consequential.

Culture depends on action that is embedded in local communities. An idioculture can be marginal or extensive, depending on the intensity, desires, and commitment of members. However, whether strong or weak, shared awareness constitutes group life. Little League baseball teams provide an instance in which groups are important, if limited in extent. Teammates use their time together to address both instrumental and expressive needs. However, the group, while powerful for the moment, does not produce extensive cultures. The case of fantasy role-play gamers reveals a culture that is more complex and multi-layered.

The sociology of culture has often emphasized the meanings of larger institutions or of society as a whole. Our claim is that culture originates in and gains power through the interaction order. Tight-knit communities provide the basis for collective memory and group solidarity. We have described group being and group belonging, both critical for a meso-sociological perspective. However, it is the content of interaction regimes that allows groups to be built. In cementing organizational continuity, local culture is crucial. Relationships matter – who would deny that? – but they matter because we give them substance through their content.

– 5 –

Bonding by Groups: The Basis for Collective Action

It isn't what we say or think that defines us, but what we do.

Jane Austen, *Sense and Sensibility*

If our actions define us more than our thoughts and words, how does a group act in concert? This deceptively simple question broaches the larger issue of collective action. Few concepts have been more valuable to the sociological study of change than that of collective action, and deservedly so. As sociology is a discipline that treats action as central and the collective as crucial, the two concepts blend together. They cannot escape each other's embrace. In this chapter, we ask how individuals can organize their behavior to produce desired outcomes, and how this occurs given the influence of various forms of social organization? How do groups motivate and energize members to act together? Bonding is key to answering these questions. Building on the previous chapters, we argue that bonding depends on a sense of being and belonging, identity, and commitment. The belief that members of a community belong – that they embrace a shared vision and common fate – enables them to work together and coordinate collaborative action. The ease of doing things together results from bonding.

Members of a community often struggle with institutional or societal change, but over time social arrangements alter because people act collectively to make it happen. We work in tandem to create new realities. In line with longstanding sociological arguments, change rarely results from the desires of a single actor or from an inchoate mass, but from a public that recognizes the importance of operating jointly. This is a point on which all sociologists implicitly embrace a localist perspective. As the English novelist Rudyard Kipling (1919: 29) memorably wrote, "For the strength of the pack is the wolf and the strength of the wolf is the pack." The individual and the group are intertwined but, more than this, a group exists because members use their shared affect to act as one. Bonding is the outcome of collective belonging. As Kipling recognized, wolves are only strong when they are in packs; humans are only strong when they have colleagues on whom they can rely. Put differently, groups depend on their members for support and to achieve desired ends; people require sturdy groups to gather sufficient power to stand against those who would oppose them. The strength and capacity for coordinated action depend on bonding and how these connections produce affiliation.

The Virtues of Affiliation

By its nature, bonding – the emotional substrate of affiliation – facilitates coordination. Coordination occurs when individuals shape their behaviors in response to those of others with the intention of carrying out a collective plan that requires mutual participation (Bratman 1992, 1993; Gilbert 1997, 2009; Tuomela 2007). We act together because we feel that the goals of others matter to us and that our goals matter to them. Coordination cannot be assumed, but is achieved through the emotional glue of joining together in a tiny public with a larger purpose: a devotion to group projects and to colleagues. In order to gain traction, collective action requires both verbal and nonverbal signaling, commitments and intentions, and scripts and negotiation. This emphasis on coordination has been central to both symbolic interaction (Scott and Lyman 1968; Blumer 1969) and conversation analysis (Sacks 1995; Schegloff 2007). Phrased in a different way, the mutual understandings that arise from an interaction order permit participants to perform as a team. Without coordination, all action will be unpredictable, and collective action will evaporate.

Commitments stem from the belief that bonding results in the satisfactions of living together. If, as we argue, the motivations that lead to bonding are a guiding principle of collective life, affection and respect will be more effective than explicit discipline. *Soft communities* – spaces that accept all those who commit to the central values of membership – operate more effectively than hard domains that demand conformity (Fine 2015). Bonding organizes social systems through the desire to be with others, accepting local practices that, when accepted, provide the basis of affective togetherness.

Several decades ago, Benedict Anderson (1991) wrote of *imagined communities*, an influential concept that ties nationalism to mutual attachment. Anderson explored the dynamics of affiliation within and with state systems, emphasizing national literatures and common languages as the basis of identification. Micro-communities are imagined as well, recognizing that those who participate often cannot and would not escape their bonds. Anderson asserted that imagined communities link the binding of individuals as a meaningful group to the acceptance of systems of governance. Imagined commitments have influence because citizens see other citizens as tied to them through their relations and cultural continuities. These linkages are especially powerful when our neighbors become metaphoric stand-ins for all within the polity.

Communal rituals such as ceremonies, pageants, or parades (Warner 1953; Lane 1981; Glassberg 1990), comprised of micro-publics gathering for an occasion, reveal bonding in action. Affiliation connects emotion to interaction on the local level but expands outward.

Settings that rely on voluntary participation are especially sensitive to those actions that bonding requires. Tiny publics, ostensibly civic scenes, may encourage political apathy, thinking that their commitment to each other only demands sociability but little else (Eliasoph 1998, 2012). In treating their group as a friendship pod, the members of many tiny publics – cliques of friendly citizens – disavow the political, distancing themselves from engagement with contesting groups with which they might come into conflict (Baiocchi et al. 2014: 40). Those who do not wish to or are not able to bond – the stranger, the hermit, or the anomic – reject the desire to shape civil society.

In addition, *defining* one's interaction partners as particular types of people supports bonding, in that it develops community meaning. This is consistent with Émile Durkheim's (1965 [1912]) belief that collective representations are crucial to communal participation, and reflects Michel Maffesoli's (1996) more recent emphasis on the organizing power of groups that he describes as tribes. Whether we accept the metaphor that tribal affiliation results from a group instinct (Chua 2018), bonding with members of a community is potent, although not universal. The hope is that each of us can find a tribe that protects us from an uncaring and heartless world (Junger 2016).

Bonding and the Culture of Movements

Groups gain strength through the commitment that they produce, even promoting the willingness to engage in costly action (Della Porta 1988; Sageman 2008). This extends beyond a feeling of belonging to a sense of bonding that then produces action in line with group desires. Affiliation in small-scale networks supports grievance frames that larger units cannot so easily generate, providing a means of overcoming fears of retribution by state actors (Gamson, Fireman, and Rytina 1982; Gould 1995; Pfaff 1996). Bonds can become so strong that, at times, even failure to achieve a goal does not produce disillusion (Summers-Effler 2010).

Once bonding has developed, it becomes salient when participants engage in actions that have risks and in which a positive outcome is uncertain. These local costs and potential benefits matter greatly in thinking about the robust commitments that groups can provide. We see this in the case of social movements. To engage willingly with others despite the dangers involved is integral to a belief that for action to have impact, social relations must generate that impact. Examining activist communities reveals a hinge between individual action and societal changes.

At times, a movement group can become, in effect, a site of performance, distilling distinct behaviors of members into focused action (List and Pettit 2011). People gain confidence from their affiliation with those who stand with them. The bonds of togetherness build power, or at least its perception. The embrace of their shared placement is more than just the result of physical closeness and reflects how identity produces collective action.

Affiliation generates powerful emotions and can inspire high-risk activism, as Jeff Goodwin (1997) found in the Huk rebellion in the Philippines. A similar, if less dramatic, phenomenon was evident in the 1970s, when consciousness-raising groups helped to create bonds that arose from the recognition of *collective* consciousness (Cassell 1977). These bonds bolstered the feminist movement, despite the barriers and mockery that young women had to overcome. Many women did not change their perspective through individual epiphanies; rather, this change occurred as groups interpreted their circumstances in mutually supportive and collectively creative ways, realizing shared troubles and developing strategies to overcome them. Although participation ebbed and flowed, leading to instability, when active these circles provided a sense of solidarity. As Durkheim (1965 [1912]) recognized, groups provide a stage where collective effervescence occurs, creating passion – and even ecstasy – in shared spaces. The challenge is to sustain affective attachment in the face of uncertainty and external threats (Bartkowski 2000). While we might debate the extent to which the character or style of interaction shapes decision-making, the bonded group often becomes a source of personal change.

For a movement to grow, to stabilize, and to gain allegiance, small units that inspire intense feelings of bonding through interaction are essential. In other words, for a movement to be effective, the bonding must both be local and extend to identification with the larger organization. Groups help to overcome the free rider problem (Olson 1965) by means of reputational and material incentives that micro-communities with tight surveillance, emotional support, and control through gossip can provide. Groups first recruit through networks, building on pre-established relations and differential association. Only later will less personal forms of mediated publicity aid in expanding membership. Although not denying the value of resources and external pressure, movements must generate the involvement of potential supporters. They must light the fire of adherents.

Close ties matter for collective action, but they can be a double-edged sword. James Kitts (2000) argues that intimate relations may inhibit participation or encourage disengagement, especially when some ties are to those outside of the group. However, when friends agree on the necessity for collaboration, a movement can thrive. Occasionally, singles attend rallies, marches, protests, or events, but more often they do so with friends and acquaintances (Aveni 1977; McPhail 1991). What appears to be a mass of protesters is often a collection of cliques, forming an evanescent "wispy community" (Fine and Van den Scott 2011): a group that gathers, interacts intensively, and then disperses, lacking a formal structure that supports routine engagement. An effective organization must support numerous tight-knit groups, operating in tandem. This is another form of bonding and a challenging one, particularly when building on crosscutting connections (Whyte 1974; Robnett 1996). When Doug McAdam (1988) speaks of Freedom High as an integral component of the civil rights movement, he refers to strategies of the organizers of Mississippi Freedom Summer for creating conditions under which disparate participants bond through classes, parties, and discussions, transcending internal divisions and surmounting external threats. A similar sociality benefitted the Ku Klux Klan, recognizing that attendance at the fiery spectacle of cross burnings serves a form of allegiance that transcends class (but not race or religion) (Blee 1992: 167; Gordon 2017).

Examinations of collective action emphasize that groups regulate entrance and exit. While addition and attrition alter the content of culture in laboratory experiments (MacNeil and Sherif 1976), the same takes place in naturally occurring groups where the backgrounds, knowledge, and expertise of recruits shift over time, creating micro-cohorts with distinct ideologies and tactics, as in the abstinence or feminist movements (Gusfield 1963; Whittier 1997). As relations change, novices embrace identification with a group and its culture, connection with those who share their space. When bonds endure, novices become old-timers.

Movements depend on internal relations for achieving (or failing to achieve) change (Blee 2012). While movements can be extensive, they are often structured through interlocking chapters or cells (Lofland and Jamison 1984), making local decision-making easier, but more challenging for a central office that must provide coordination. In this sense, movements are reticulated organizations (Gerlach and Hine 1970), with local units that have distinctive cultures, resources, leadership, and outcomes (Reger 2002; Andrews et al. 2010). We find this national headquarters / local chapter structure in associations as diverse as the Communist Party of America, the Tea Party movement, Mothers Against Drunk Driving, and the NAACP. Depending on the desire of core leaders or a steering committee to coordinate action or institute surveillance, the connection among independent chapters may be strong or loosely coupled.

Groups as Sites for Collective Action

Groups allow for a variety of forms of collaboration and bonding, encouraging members to act jointly on projects that they believe to be beneficial for themselves and others. This justifies social movement involvement. The intense local commitment among friends and colleagues limits top-down control by elites with more resource power. The question becomes how and to what extent do tight-knit small groups shape society? How can tiny publics challenge those outside of their boundaries? Can they alter institutions and shape politics? The local sociology perspective argues that, through the power of affiliation, tiny publics are the building blocks through which societies change and address what are believed to be collective problems. We discuss the extensions of groups in chapter 7, but here we address groups as producing collective action.

Voluntary communities create the possibility of civic virtue, or, depending on one's perspective, civic vice. In some cases, as with cafes or neighborhood taverns (Walsh 2003; Erickson 2009) that are places of apolitical sociability, the concern is to support colleagues in the face of personal problems. Here we find action and communal concern, but not collective action. Groups, when they define themselves as primarily sociable or when they feel that the problems that they face are overwhelming, may choose to avoid activism, even while caring for others. The commitments of sociability are often separate from public duty.

Collective angst over highly local issues can occur at the same time as broader political apathy. Nina Eliasoph (1998) discovered this phenomenon when observing friends ostensibly focused on community goals, such as drug abuse or environmental threats. Groups may choose not to think globally or to act locally, accepting the pleasures of camaraderie as primary, prioritizing bonding over change.

While we might see the generation of a civic culture as dependent on the idiosyncratic choices of individuals or on the large movement of masses, the presence of groups birthed the foundations of the contemporary public sphere from the late seventeenth to early nineteenth centuries (Calhoun 1982). A well-tempered civil society requires the local regulation of social relations. Ongoing interaction scenes are the basis for public engagement and collective action. Consequently, communities must set aside domains – physical places or online spaces – that permit events that are often (although not inevitably) marked by rituals that become signs of bonding. To perform together is to feel secure.

Whether these spaces are provided by communal institutions or not, gathering points lead to fluid communication. If we consider the bases of civil society, it is natural to point to tiny locales such as the coffee house (Back and Polisar 1983), the lodge (Koselleck 1988: 70–92; Kaufman 1999), the club (Amann 1975: 33–77), the salon (Giesen 2001: 223–4), the literary society (Habermas 1989: 34), the book club (Long 2003), or, today, a meet-up or online Facebook group. Mario Small (2009: v) described the empowerment provided by urban daycare centers (at first considered instrumental venues without much civic impact). These institutions provide resources that allow parents to achieve goals that their limited incomes would not permit.

In addition, public meetings and community institutions embed citizens in civil society. We see this both in political gatherings in urban neighborhoods in Brazil and in town meetings in New England (Baiocchi 2003; Bryan 2004). Although Alexis de Tocqueville (1966: 662–6) is often treated as a writer who emphasized expansive forms of association, he recognized that these projects can be "very minute" and "carry out [a] vast multitude of lesser undertakings." Minute associations operate more like a committee than a movement, but, large or small, they motivate collective action among the committed, sometimes targeting opponents.

The small group is a domain in which people commit to communities and institutions, motivating them to act in ways that they might not do without interpersonal support – whether this entails storming the US Capitol after a MAGA rally or burning a city police station during a Black Lives Matter protest. Whether one is appalled by these groups or agrees with them, our point is analytic, emphasizing that too often the affective ties of protesters have been marginalized in treatments of the public sphere and political movements. This comes at the cost of ignoring the practical, meso-level explanation of how linkages between individuals and larger society are formed.

Civic Spaces and Collective Action

The existence of places in which committed friends gather builds local politics. As Ari Adut (2012: 238) argues, every public sphere requires a spatial core where communion is possible. For Adut, these are sites of publicity and public awareness. A shared space permits a stage for performance by a troupe of actors (Adut 2012: 244; Allen 2015: 178, 181). But both the crowd and the recluse depend on spatial resources, even if nothing much develops until there is a recognition of bonding. Civic spaces transform action to acting in the presence of an audience that sees the performance as a meaningful expression of a shared vision.

For audiences, these performances may be fun and seductive. But all is not delight. Just as groups provide a space for collective action and organized debate, they also permit rivalry or conflict (a topic of chapter 6). This recognition that emotional engagement produces not only bonding but breakage cautions us against treating thorny patches as rose arbors. Co-presence may reveal divisions and encourage conflict within and between groups. James Jasper (2004: 13) speaks of the "band of brothers" dilemma, the recognition that bonds that are too tight in spaces with limited resources may quickly become exclusionary or divided. These internal boundaries raise the question of whom group action protects: the tightly linked in-group or all those present.

Despite the potential for conflict, co-presence is essential for any well-functioning society. Being together both reflects and contributes to mutual concern. We find this in the influential ethnographic trope of the *corner* as the stage on which the life of the community is displayed (Whyte 1943; Liebow 1967; Anderson 1979). The corner is a place where people are known, expected, teased, and cared for, and in which practices are well established. Villages or kibbutzim serve much the same purpose in that there is a pressure – admittedly, one not always successful – for routine interaction to be treated as friendly and secure. This allows participants to support common goals. Perhaps we might claim that interactional spaces, more than parallel minds, create moral orders.

When group bonds are secure and the boundaries against disruption are strong, we can speak of safe spaces. Religious buildings serve as a case in point. Houses of worship must be comforting places of community (Hart 2001: 35). It is hard to imagine a Church – a set of institutionally sponsored beliefs – without edifices in which beliefs are spoken. Lacking a place for congregants to gather for devotional practices, faith could easily wither. As Iddo

Tavory (2016: 64) argues, synagogues are compassionate clubs, providing the possibility of "synagogue life." Their clubbiness permits participants to work together on charitable enterprises. For religious congregations, believers are not only orthodox (sharing beliefs), but orthoprax (worshipping together). These shared commitments permit churches to become social welfare organizations. Jeffrey Guhin (2016) argues that some religions – Islam, for example – emphasize the shared performance of ritual (doing faith together), although, admittedly, discourse bolstering orthodoxy (talking together) in other religions, such as conservative Protestantism, may strengthen relations as well.

To defend their interactional order, some groups guard semi-private spaces or privatize public space (Duneier 1999). For example, the large event "Burning Man," composed of a network of friendship knots and producing emergent organization, establishes a temporary public–private space in the wilds of the Nevada desert (Chen 2009), establishing a wispy community in the sagebrush. As Marcus Britton (2008: 442) finds, groups may claim "regular spots"; these locations shape identity and permit private (or even stigmatized) behaviors in public. One such group revealed greater racial consciousness on a street corner, owning the space as Black men, than they did in a soup kitchen that rejected the expression of overt racial identification.

Likewise, groups may be accessible to outsiders in certain spots while holding closed gatherings elsewhere for those most committed (Coco and Woodward 2007). For example, we find bounded spaces among innovative and tightly knit scientific groups. In the case of the Resilience Alliance – an interdisciplinary network seeking to revolutionize the science of ecology and the understanding of environmental change – holding small, intense meetings in isolated locales was vital. This "Island Time" became a central creative and bonding mechanism for their movement. The place itself may lack significance until the presence of the group gives it meaning, as we discuss with regard to activities of amateur mushroom hunters. As John Parker and Edward Hackett (2012) point out, these scientific spaces provide "hot spots and hot moments." In recruiting those with shared interests, they become magnet places (Farrell 2001; Corte 2013) or truth spots (Gieryn 2018).

Taken together, these examples suggest a basic ecological and emotional reality, one that is central to our argument: spatial structures encourage (or sometimes discourage) the interactions necessary for bonding. The mingling of people, channeled by the obdurate structures of urban architecture, builds (or prevents) coordination. When friends and acquaintances meet, civic action can result. For example, Dingxin Zhao (2001: 147) reports of the 1989 Tiananmen Square protest, "I found many [interviews and memoirs] in the form 'I walked down the road and saw X . . . and then I decided to do Z.'" While Zhao considers this an unplanned and spontaneous protest, it nevertheless emphasizes the importance of meeting places (DeLand 2018). Spatial contexts and constraints permit spontaneous protest (Snow and Moss 2014: 1146). The proximity of Beijing's universities, the walled separation of these universities from the city, and the densely located dormitories encouraged collective action that might have been perceived as too risky in the absence of this layout. Today, gathering places are found in virtual space, a reality to which we return in chapter 7.

These micro-worlds are what Ray Oldenburg (1989) terms "third places": sites of voluntary, communal belonging, apart from the more formal structures of work and home. The ecological features of neighborhoods affect the bonding that develops within. Streets, cul-de-sacs, parks, and plazas make gatherings more or less likely (Grannis 2009). Regular interactions produce a recognition of community. Christopher Browning and his colleagues (Browning et al. 2017) discovered that neighborhoods where residents interact more frequently – revealing dense networks – show higher levels of efficacy. Although active neighborhood networks create allegiance, they often involve structural segregation and assume a similarity of residents that creates a tight-knit identity and an imagined – and exclusionary – comity. A case in point is those all too frequent incidents in which White residents call the police to confront African Americans for the mere offense of being out of place – Black in a White space (Anderson 2015) – suggesting that, in the eyes of those offended, neighborly affiliations do not apply.

For groups that face exclusion and sanctions for crossing boundaries, small acts of resistance are a crucial form of contestation in repressive regimes (Johnston 2006). This is especially so where surveillance is unlikely and in which personal connections are strong. Privacy generates "actor constitution," the willing participation in groups that counter repression, despite the risk of sanctioning by authorities. The hush arbors of African American slave religion in which resistance could be spoken, apart from those who would enforce control, demonstrate that closed spaces can undercut authority (Scott 1987).

These free spaces appear in studies of oppositional movements in democratic polities (Evans and Boyte 1986; Futrell and Simi 2004) as well as in struggles against authoritarian regimes. Forms of commitment linking discourse and action are common in engaged publics (Mische and White 1998; Emirbayer and Sheller 1999), each of which has a distinctive style of interaction and a local normative order. Participants assume that others share a remembered history, an empathic concern, and a recognition of strong relations. These intimate spaces, communities of sympathy and experience (hair salons, coffee houses, reading groups, poker nights, or church suppers), support civil society, as they may be where politics is discussed among friends and colleagues (Walsh 2003).

Local sociology draws from a microsociological perspective that is implicit in the literature on collective action. The idea of associationism, with its implications about the strength of civil society (Kaufman 1999), affirms the centrality of interaction. Local communities and the places in which they exist provide a foundation for society. Small groups and the bonds that they provide are cause and consequence of civic engagement. The attachment of individuals to those groups in which they participate reveals that embedded identities can build powerful local communities.

Thinking in Cases

To understand how bonding produces collective action, we present data from ethnographic studies of a club for mushroom collectors (the Minnesota Mycological Society) (Fine 1998) and a progressive activist organization of senior citizens (that we name Chicago Seniors Together) (Fine, in press). These are sites in which affiliation is important and leads to members acting in concert. Each group created events that invited participation, although the activists performed their events in public spaces. In both cases, building on group cultures, bonding depends on a being and belonging, identity and commitment.

The examination of the mushrooming community in *Morel Tales: The Culture of Mushrooming* was based on four years of research in Minnesota and at national forays. The goal was to understand how people came to appreciate and define nature and develop a sense of environmental ethics. This did not arise from individual experience, but through the bonding that developed from being "in nature." Based on togetherness, environmental ethics was a *social* project, engaged in by a tight-knit community. That these naturalists held meetings, organized forays, and attended national and regional gatherings was crucial. The Minnesota Mycological Society consisted of about

200 members with two dozen regular participants, fairly evenly divided between men and women. Although their actions were not expressly a form of political engagement, they were no less collective.

In contrast, Chicago Seniors Together, described in *Fair Share: Senior Activism, Tiny Publics, and the Culture of Resistance*, had a clear political agenda. This organization, devoted to changing policy in a progressive direction, was observed for a period of 30 months. The goal was to understand how political engagement operated within a group context and, in particular, to examine how age and vulnerability affected activism. Chicago Seniors Together had some 500 members, primarily senior citizens, with most between 65 and 90 years of age. About two-thirds of the active members were female and many were White, despite the strong desire for a multi-racial organization. As with the mushroomers, only a few dozen members were active. While the coalition held social events, their primary goal was to organize demonstrations and rallies, conduct phone banks, collect petitions, and meet with politicians. Their related political action organization endorsed liberal candidates and promoted a partisan progressive agenda. A feeling of bonding, encouraged by the staff and leading members, was intended to translate into collective action.

As many organizations recognize to their regret, it is all too easy for a once-thriving voluntary organization to disintegrate (Messinger 1955). Those who lead the organization must find times and places for active engagement. Providing satisfaction and education is crucial for voluntary groups, as those who participate hope to benefit from their involvement. This requires leaders not merely to publicize events for their followers, but to encourage collective action through a sense of togetherness.

Enjoying Fungi Together

Leisure groupings are, at their core, places where participants feel that their commitment to each other brings satisfaction. In the case of mushroom collectors – and many other groups – given the low exit cost, the desires of members must be met continuously. These gatherings have the problem of voluntary organizations: how to cement members to the community despite the expense of money and time. Fun is the goal, but it must be a shared fun in which all can participate, even if hierarchies of authority and control exist. One mushroom club leader commented to the assembled members, "The first and foremost objective on my list is to have fun! . . . I'm really looking forward to a year of putting the 'fun' in fungi . . . with you!"

A key feature of small voluntary organizations that engage in serious leisure (Stebbins 2006) concerns making available assets and arenas for action. This connects with resource mobilization theory, which argues that, for collective action to be successful, the organization must provide opportunities for engagement (McCarthy and Zald 1977). While we can think about the provisioning of knowledge or identity symbols, spaces are essential for bonding. Providing arenas for collective engagement – staging areas for allegiance – is crucial for the health of any organization.

Although meetings serve this purpose, we focus on special occasions that the organization established to promote bonding. The annual banquet, held in the mushroom-free winter, was one such occasion, and a surprisingly complicated one: One year the hotel at which the banquet was scheduled refused to permit members to bring in prepared food (perhaps especially mushrooms) for fear of liability. Lacking the banquet's main attraction, members judged the event to be a failure in promoting camaraderie.

Creating events can be a challenge, but, when successful, they cement the community. For the mushroomers, forays were an especially salient occasion of organized sociability, times and places where members gathered to collect mushrooms together. Here, as with much collective action, the devil is in the details. Those charged with responsibility had to select a location, choose a date on which mushrooms were likely to be fruiting, gain permission from park authorities or private landowners, provide directions and maps, choose experts to help to identify the mushrooms collected, and then promote the event. Finally, they had to hope for rain before the date, and sun that morning. These occasions were crucial for connecting members of the Minnesota Mycological Society to the club and to each other, and for inspiring anecdotes that became part of the lore of the group, encouraging members to continue to spend time together.

For the Minnesota club, a half-dozen events were planned in the fall, including a multi-day foray. These forms of collective action required the central engagement of a few, and allowed many to be free riders as long as they publicly expressed their gratitude. Indeed, in many leisure organizations, new members are allowed this free ride, but those who return are often encouraged (or pressured) to volunteer through a kind of bait-and-switch. A group does not require a king, but depends on a court: a core group whose efforts at collaboration produce the occasions for collective sociability and emotional intensity. Requests to help the organization to arrange occasions are hard to refuse if the entreaty is from a friend. Collaboration depends upon the recognition of shared responsibility, producing affection.

Forays serve a dual purpose. First, they provide spaces of leisure, permitting those forms of collective activity that participants desire. Second, equally significant for the tensile strength of the organization, the event is a social situation in which friendship ties are established. In other words, occasions work both for the members and for the group. With regard to the first purpose, an organizer pointed out, "The Northeastern Mycological Foray is all about the opportunity to eat, live, and breathe mushrooms for four days." However, he might have added that it allows you to eat, live, and talk *with mushroomers* for four days. Forays were social as well as scientific affairs.

Participants photographed mushrooms and mushroomers, sometimes having the latter hold the former. Further, tokens permitted a material form of memory in this "great big party." Exploring the woods, often an empty space from a human perspective, with those for whom one cares, revealed the presence of affective ties. As one friend pointed out about the experience of a foray, "Besides the joy of finding them is the joy of sharing them." Despite the challenge of organizing, collective events justify togetherness for voluntary groups.

While not a political group as such, mushroomers discussed relevant political and environmental issues. As individuals, they were concerned about climate change, pollution, or development, but they did not engage in protests that might have promoted a solution. Their collective action was in the woods and fields. In this sense, the mushroomers studied are similar to the groups – politically apathetic anti-drug groups and country music fanciers – described by Nina Eliasoph (1998). Sociability was a sufficient justification for their involvement, and foraging became their collective activity.

Resisting Together

The absence of explicit political action among mushroomers, despite their inchoate concerns, contrasts directly with the engagements of Chicago Seniors Together. This group believed – at least in a general sense – in the forms of progressive politics developed by the Chicago activist Saul Alinsky (1971). Alinsky argued for action to incite confrontation, and selected fights that he considered winnable. Groups, even while thinking globally, must act locally.

This is desirable in theory, but it requires participants who are willing to give of their time and energy, and at times face costs that result from their political actions if authorities are able to sanction them. Such a movement requires strong commitment, backed by the motivation that social bonds provide. Unlike the mushroom club,

Chicago Seniors Together, funded by contributions from members and grants from like-minded foundations, hired a staff of between five and seven that provided the organizing backbone, collaborating with the most active members, defined as the leaders. However, for collective action to succeed, staff members had the responsibility of ensuring that actions were well coordinated.

During the period of observation, staff planned a continuing set of activities, keeping seniors committed. However, the organization also had to cope with a churn of members and staff as engagement was often temporary and unstable. Despite the changing membership, staff and leaders attempted to create a sense that each member depended on the others to achieve their political ends. Joining Chicago Seniors Together suggested that one was working collaboratively to better society. Their bonding was evident at the opening of meetings that began with a "relational exercise," in which each attendee briefly described an activity in which they had participated or a belief that they held. This provided evidence that they knew each other and, by sharing, that they could count on each other.

Like the Minnesota Mycological Society, Chicago Seniors Together organized events that promoted solidarity. However, these events differed in important ways. First, the staff had considerable input in their planning, even if working groups and the senior leaders on the Board of Directors had some measure of authority. Perhaps the crucial difference was that, rather than looking inward to provide satisfaction for individual members, the goal was to shape public perceptions and discomfort political enemies. Whether this happened was not always clear, but it was desired.

Consider one of the most memorable events that Chicago Seniors Together organized. Whether this collective action had any direct and tangible effects on public policy might be doubted, but it strengthened the community. This was a demonstration held at the office of a prominent Republican

Congressman in a neighboring state. The organization rented buses to travel as a group for 45 minutes in the middle of March, on what turned out to be a snowy, blustery day. As the inches accumulated, the snowfall was routinely referred to as a "blizzard," warmly exaggerating the chill for dramatic effect and a sense of having jointly and joyously overcome obstacles. As one senior shared, "What I carry with me is how empowering it was to see our people out there with their best canes, walkers and prosthetic legs in fourteen-inch lake effect snow. It wasn't a weak demonstration, but a powerful one. People spontaneously gave us what we needed. The more I did it, the more empowering it was." A 90-year-old proudly explained, "We're not twenty years old anymore." Another recalled, "In a strange kind of way, the snow worked in our favor," making the protest more dramatic and providing "images that the media used in two states." They were heroic for braving the elements despite their frailties.

Dramatic events, solidified through the right stories, freeze a moment in time, and, when shared in the proper location, generate soulful collective memory and the moral authority that movements require. Emplotment is a tool that is crucial to collective action (Ricoeur 1984). Movements thrive when members transform events into experience, experience into narrative, and narrative back into action. When this occurs and when participants share stories, bonding and commitment to movement goals increase.

Participants build engagement by presenting the group as a legitimate generator of collective action. These forms of *eventful experience* are crucial as they utilize memorable moments for purposes of cohesion. Members see powerful groups produce a linked trajectory, a shared future, and an agreed-on narrative (Farrell 2001; Parker and Hackett 2012), crucial resources for the continuation of the group despite centrifugal forces.

The linkage of levels that integrates personal experience and public demonstrations is crucial for recognizing how individuals acting jointly and remembering together motivate collective action. For movement organizations such as Chicago Seniors Together, bonding begins on the inside to promote the desire for public activities, and, in turn, those public activities increase bonding, creating a cycle of engagement.

Group Bonding

In this chapter, we emphasize how bonding supports collective action. Whatever power we might give to the idea of the group – and we award great emphasis to this meso-level of analysis – groups are composed of individuals, tied together by commitments and social relations. However, groups only work when individuals are organized. The actions of participants form a social jigsaw. It is not merely that individuals connect their lines of action, as Herbert Blumer (1969) suggested; something deeper is at work. What must happen is for individuals to join together on projects. We see their collaboration when mushroomers coordinate tasks in making a foray a success, but also when they work together in identifying specimens when no one person has complete mycological knowledge. In a similar way, for activists to organize a demonstration, tasks must fit together or be jointly performed.

We make a further argument. There is an emotional substrate to this process. Bonding is crucial to a sense of being a collective entity, and, in turn, collective action increases the salience of bonding. How is this possible? Bonding helps to explain why people do not simply decide as individuals to act however they think proper. The local sociology perspective argues that the activation of commitment is crucial. In chapter 2, we emphasized the importance of identity arising out of group placement. In chapter 3, we suggested that belonging produces commitment to the group. In chapter 4, we recognized that groups are domains of meaning. Here we argue that bonds promote collective action, allowing the group to reach inward and outward.

Understanding the dynamics of bonding is critical in that it treats the group as an action arena, not merely a comforting commune. Whether the group focuses on serving the interests of members, or on inserting itself into public debates as a form of social pressure, joint engagement is essential. Sociality makes collective action possible.

– PART III –
THE GROUP IN THE WORLD

– 6 –

Battling Groups: The Minuet of Conflict and Control

> People who treat other people as less than human must not be surprised when the bread they have cast on the waters comes floating back to them, poisoned.
>
> James Baldwin, *No Name in the Street*

What is the place of conflict and control in local sociology? As James Baldwin correctly explains, oppression and hostility are too often part of social life, and insults and offense creates further insult and offense. However, by emphasizing the beneficial properties of group life, it might seem as though we privilege smooth harmony over rough contention. The placid notion is that if people are sufficiently local, sharing a world, they will get along. This satisfying approach suggests a belief in positive sociology. While tempting, we must guard against this claim. All too often people struggle to harmonize. Even more importantly, it is often the case that change is only possible when groups diverge. Poisoned bread demands better baking.

In this chapter, we argue that examining life on the meso-level does not presume an absence of conflict. Indeed, tensions within and between groups are common, the achievement of control is not a given, authority can be a source of oppression, and conflict can prompt change. Moreover, challenges can generate a sense of order, replacing cooperation as a source of stability. Anyone who has participated in tiny publics realizes that they can be contentious, even splitting or dissolving. The group is a crucible in which a full range of emotions is present. In the extreme, communities can be riven if competing cultures are formed (Martin 1992; Weeks 2003) or if neighbors are seen as rivals to be defeated.

While these conflicts are often undesirable, we ask whether and how disruption organizes group life. Just as cultures can be disputed with the potential of fragmenting an interaction order, others can treat these spaces as sites of control, using rewards and punishments to achieve outcomes reflecting how they believe communal life should operate. Both protest groups and those who police them have interests in the dynamics of collective action. So, too, do provocateurs, complainers, and those who muzzle dissent.

In what follows, we describe the effects of divisions, disruptions, and dissent within groups, and also the dynamics of disciplining forces. Underlying this is the question of how organizations – congeries of groups – develop a culture from networks within, a key insight of the localist approach known as "inhabited institutionalism." Instead of assuming a world that is free of contestation, viewing the world through a meso-lens reveals how conflict and control shape outcomes in a dynamic way.

Conflict and Control

Is harmony the natural state of group life? Is consensus necessarily a moral value? Under what circumstances is contention a legitimate alternative? Is smooth agreement more virtuous than spiky debate? If so, what is the effect on a local community of the desire for comity? Can disruption support an interaction order in place of cooperation?

From Erving Goffman's (1967) face-saving rituals of deference and demeanor to Randall Collins' (2004) interaction ritual chains; from conversation analysts' emphasis on repair (Schegloff 1992) to Anselm Strauss' (1978) belief in the weight of the negotiated order, microsociologists have often conceived of accord as an ideal of interpersonal relations. Yet, despite a shared commitment to process, incorporating conflict and contention may provide tensile strength for local communities, birthing needed change or inspiring renewal. Erving Goffman wrote of a "veneer of consensus" by which he meant that, through impression management, we express the belief that our communal activity must be characterized by an assumption of agreement, no matter how illusory. However, despite this preferred perspective, veneers can cover a splintered base. Goffman awarded priority to coordination over dispute, but, as Lewis Coser (1956) emphasized, conflict may be desirable, too.

Few deny that a willingness to compromise facilitates civility, reduces transaction costs, and encourages mutual appreciation. But how does commitment occur when differing perspectives are embedded in local practices? Ideally, members share a perspective. Otherwise, what had been a group or what might potentially become one falls apart or never coheres.

It is easy to assume that, in the face of heavy moral traffic, people search for exit ramps to avoid collisions. The desire for comity explains how respectful dramaturgical practices signal the presence of a good society (Kuzmics 1991; Smith 2006: 25–6). But there is something unsatisfying in proclaiming conclaves as kumbaya, or gatherings as Quaker meetings. While every theoretical tradition recognizes the possibility of disruptive moments, these breaches are often treated as a failure of the social rather than as being integral to it. Such "conflicts of interpretation" – or what Isaac Reed (2006: 149, 156) terms "shipwrecks" – can produce aggressive responses, temporary or ongoing.

Focusing on smooth relations may prevent an appreciation of how conflict can inspire or encourage. Contentious politics can be productive politics, provoking needed change. In a similar fashion, harmonious governance can be oppressive, preserving the privileges of the powerful. Confrontation can be a bracing challenge (Baiocchi et al. 2014: 70). Although disputes may not be inherent to group life, they are a crucial mechanism by which groups adjust to the presence of multiple perspectives in a kaleidoscopic world.

By reconceiving what had once been taken as unproblematic, conflict sparks problem solving, even while opening the local community to the risk of disintegration. Although the continued smooth functioning of a group through interpersonal strategies is a central skill, as Neil Fligstein (2001) suggests, establishing productive disharmony is also a skill. Judith Butler (2006) reminds us that dissensus and the recognition of troubles are performative and potentially persuasive. When performance is provocation, actors demand collective rethinking, examining unconsidered personal preferences (Alexander 2017).

Interpersonal harmony need not be a desideratum, and conflict can be a valid strategy in roiling an established social order. Instability, when it avoids epistemic turmoil, can prevent stasis. This, however, is not a paean to disputes. Even if disruptions *can*, at times, generate communal benefits, this does not mean that contestation, like consensus, inevitably strengthens an interaction order. Much depends on how the debate is managed.

Local Conflicts and the Order of Battle

What are the circumstances under which harmony becomes conflict, or conflict becomes harmony? Part of the answer involves the authority of influential participants to define collective identity, returning to our discussion in chapter 2. The group is the crucible for the development of a shared moral identity, shaped by common beliefs and intersecting lines of action, and rejecting identities imposed from the outside. Michael Haedicke (2012), for example, finds that, in responding to external challenges, those running natural food co-ops bolstered a shared culture to manage contentious decisions that had the potential to split the group. While small communities do not always succeed in coalescing, given the heated pressure of some disputes, reconsideration of values and traditions can produce a newly negotiated consensus.

Treating conflict as variable within an interaction order suggests whether a group will welcome new members, how demanding the process of initiation will be, and the extent to which the group will tolerate the presence of outsiders. For example, in observing Australian pagans, Angela Coco and Ian Woodward (2007: 479) found a sharp divide between those who wanted the culture to be esoteric, remaining true to a set of core beliefs, and others who hoped to promote pagan beliefs and values to a wider audience, even if the culture had to be diluted as it became more accessible. They debated whether more outreach and an enlarged community was desirable. They all recognized popular cultural representations that might have had broad appeal. Yet those who valued the esoteric scorned those who sought to share, suggesting that they wished to transform pagan beliefs into an embrace of "fluffy bunnies," changing serious commitment to something warm and fuzzy. The latter felt that the former were obtuse and unwilling to spread the word of something that they found meaningful. Both sides wished to embrace a collective identity that they claimed captured the group's ethos, but in different ways and to different degrees.

These tensions are common. We see them in many religions and ideological battles, past and present. How Marxist must a communist be? How Randian a libertarian? Despite such tensions, experimental research finds that conflict does not inevitably lead to group dysfunction. Stephen Benard and Pat Barclay (2020) discovered that some forms of friction – what they describe as democratic competition – may increase the amount of public goods and bolster efficiency (admittedly by increasing deception to achieve these positive outcomes on occasion). Their experimental studies reveal that conflict is not separate from order but contributes to it. Order may be generated through continuing disagreements that can be either negotiable or disabling. Respectful competition benefits stable organizations, such as church congregations with the resources and commitments to manage congenial disputes as they build a compassionate community, despite differing viewpoints on how that should be achieved (Becker 1999; Putnam and Campbell 2010). However, lacking either resources or commitments, a group is likely to split or dissolve.

Competing meanings within group cultures allow for disruption. Even in the case of ongoing conflict, strong affiliation may prevent the dissolution of communal life. The resolution of disagreement – temporarily or permanently – depends on the navigation of challenges to a moral domain in light of an established local culture. We see this in research by Craig Calhoun (1982) on British nineteenth-century radicalism. Calhoun finds that class struggles during the Industrial Revolution were nurtured by the commitments of those within local craft communities to resist changes brought about by external economic pressures while maintaining their culture. Intimacy, coupled with a recognition of threats to workers' lifeworlds, provided the basis for opposition to those who promoted a new factory system.

In any struggle, enduring success requires a balance between the array of diverse local cultures and the control and coordination provided by a centralized authority. This reflects a tension between discipline and autonomy, pragmatism and authenticity. Movements that promote change through activist chapters hope to persuade their colleagues of the need for a uniform sensibility, while encouraging commitments that arise from close personal ties. This is not always easy, as is evident in the Tea Party movement's rapid rise and collapse. Tea Parties generated strong attachment, shared emotions, and joint activities among like-minded neighbors. This was lost when the groups were "organized" by larger entities, such as FreedomWorks, diminishing both the authority and the draw of neighborly units. A grassroots movement was posed against Astroturf outsiders that vitiated cooperative energy, local creativity, and committed friendships.

By itself, the absence of conflict does not imply the justice of any particular claim; what is treated as "justice" belongs to an interpretive field that recognizes divergent meanings. Challenges to established systems are found in the toolkit of group life, particularly at uncertain moments when new ideologies arise (Swidler 1986). In unsettled times, the taken-for-granted comprehension of the once comfortable social order is challenged, and newly established implicit rules are needed. Unsettled times unsettle groups. Some communities hold to a firm epistemological consensus that is supported by a robust local culture, while others are in a continual process of cognitive churning and emotional ferment. However, whatever the diverse rituals of argumentation, some rules to manage contention must arise to allow sociability to continue, otherwise the rupture will be beyond repair.

Conflict can strengthen internal bonds in response to outsiders who are seen as hostile. As it does this, it can oblige the group to coalesce against threats that are taken as real. Moreover, given these internal forces, perceived opposition can serve as a bridging mechanism in building alliances among groups with similar styles, values, or goals. In this way, disruption can be a strategy used by social actors at particular moments – neither inherently valuable nor eternally destructive. Ultimately, conflict is integrated into local cultures, producing what anthropologist Bruno Latour (2005) writes of as the reassembly of the social. The social is always in play, but the play can be rough.

Controlling Action

To maintain itself, every tiny public depends on a recognized interaction order that enforces *standards* and demands *predictability*, even if members chafe at such constraints. Social control is part of all organized social systems. Systems of power inevitably depend on chains of relations and methods of interpretation (Reed 2017). Norms (actions that communities treat as morally or socially proper) and routines (expectations that create predictable circuits of action) are essential to any theory of control, group-based or otherwise.

Focusing on order within group cultures allows us to address Thomas Hobbes' challenge of how societies can be organized in the face of individual desires and demands. Hobbes postulates a centralized and extended institution – the Leviathan – that enforces constraints, limiting the choices of individuals. Hobbes erases group culture on both sides of the social control boundary: the local meanings of the powerful and of the regulated. Can individuals be free while still embracing the order that expectations provide and on which ongoing institutions insist?

We believe that the answer to this question is yes, but the answer is only visible in shifting our gaze to the combination of liberty and order in local worlds. We must avoid thinking only of the linkage of individual and institution without considering the interaction orders and group cultures that serve as a hinge. It is not just that groups link the micro and the macro; rather, the meso-level has properties that in its local authority permit forms of control separate from the individual and the institutional. Local communities may be characterized by authority from above, resistance from below, or by agreement from the sides. Each is a form of discipline, dependent on collaboration. That groups operate in a behavioral space situated between persons and structures is crucial to enacting order. When societies work efficiently and amiably, control is implicit, and welcomed, as it supports a shared desire for moral propriety. When this happens, constraints do not depend on the whims of the powerful; they reflect communal choices.

For their own protection, groups often erect barriers to participation by those defined as disruptive, disagreeable, or resistant – and may choose to sanction them. As legal scholar Robert Ellickson (1991) argues, local control is the ideal, an imagined utopia. This is the moral weight of "order without law." Political scientist James Scott (2012: 30) speaks of a "vernacular order" that challenges the "official order." In small-scale social systems, such as roommate dyads (Emerson 2008), committees (Haug 2013), or workplace meetings (Hallett, Harger, and Eder 2009), informal control supports congenial relations, encouraging communal remediation (Morrill 1995).

In other cases, particularly those that are far more repressive, external groups, often agents of the state, establish mechanisms of control, sometimes involving harshly punitive sanctions aimed at disrupting those thought dangerous (Reedy, Gastil, and Gabbay 2013). This direct control from above is used by authoritarian regimes, such as the People's Republic of China, when, during the Cultural Revolution, the state assembled groups of five to eight citizens – *hsiao-tsu* – to indoctrinate and coerce them through the performance of political rituals as well as heightened interpersonal surveillance (Whyte 1974). State actors often have resources that allow them to create such social spaces. However, the control of group members works most effectively when authorities discreetly glove power. When citizens accept this subtle ordering, they bow to the domination of the mighty.

In conceptualizing the local as the linkage between individual actors and extended structures, localism bridges social psychology, cultural studies, and institutional or organizational sociology. As prominent as culture has become in the social sciences, this was not always so.

Prior to the *cultural turn* of the early 1980s (Friedland and Mohr 2004), scholars rarely attempted to explain organizational traditions (Morrill 2008: 15). Eventually, culture became integral to understanding the dynamics of social control. While some scholars treat the concept as a macro-characteristic of societies (e.g., Munch and Smelser 1993; Meyer and Jepperson 2000), because most communities are characterized by cognitive, affective, and behavioral diversity, these analyses are invariably imprecise. With regard to organizational sociology, examples of the macro-use of culture include discussions of "rationalized myths" (Meyer and Rowan 1977) or "institutional logics" (Friedland and Alford 1991). In this view, individuals are shaped through their positions in an institutional field, rather than through an interaction order. In contrast, we believe that group culture is a means through which actors make claims, negotiate, and create affiliation.

Conflict and Control in Inhabited Institutionalism

If organizational sociology has not always focused on groups and their interactions – emphasizing instead the structural skeleton or the surrounding ecology – scholars have increasingly recognized the microfoundations of institutional life (Barley 2008; Powell and Colyvas 2008; Fine and Hallett 2014). The approach known as "inhabited institutionalism" (Scully and Creed 1997; Hallett and Ventresca 2006) mines these theoretical veins, including those that focus on individual agency (Battilana 2006), the interests of organizational entrepreneurs (DiMaggio 1988; Hardy and Maguire 2008; Battilana, Leca, and Boxenbaum 2009), the skills of those who reshape organizations (Fligstein and McAdam 2012), as well as "institutional work." This latter is defined as the "purposive action of individuals and organizations aimed at creating, maintaining, and disrupting institutions" (Lawrence and Suddaby 2006: 216).

We do not dismiss these approaches but, compared to inhabited institutionalism, they are less attuned to interaction, groups, and the creation of a self-referential culture. Inhabited institutionalism relies heavily on the recognition of local practices and interactional styles. This incorporates the negotiated order perspective that is characteristic of contemporary symbolic interactionism (McGinty 2014). Inhabited institutionalism directs our attention to how organizational practices draw on meanings established by interacting groups, and the micropolitics and conflicts therein (Binder 2007; Aurini 2012; Everitt 2012; Nunn 2014).

In thinking about these struggles, inhabited institutionalism stresses interaction because it recognizes that actors must *collaborate* to achieve their divergent interests (Hallett and Hawbaker 2020). Moreover, the goals that are to be achieved are neither certain nor unambiguous, but emerge through negotiation. In other words, interests are rarely a given, and micropolitics are linked to an interpretive process found within social relations (Reed 2017). It is through interactions with others that "interests" take shape and come to have particular meanings as a basis for ongoing action (Blumer 1969; Hallett 2010). Although scholars commonly speak of "competing interests" and "conflicts of interests," such language is a gloss that covers interactional struggles over meaning (Hallett and Hawbaker 2021).

Because preferences are socially and often locally defined, power and control may not be anti-democratic or even inherently coercive (Lukes 2005) – although that is often the case. While it is true that organizations have a hierarchical structure and that formal authority relations flow from these structures, there is also an underlying dimension of informal symbolic power. Whereas formal authority is typically obvious, symbolic power is more subtle. In organizational contexts, symbolic power constitutes the ability to define the situation such that people cooperate without thinking of alternatives (Bourdieu 1991; Hallett 2003).

Whereas formal authority is evident on organizational charts and in positional titles, symbolic power is found in the "shadowland of informal interaction" (Selznick 1966 [1949]: 260) that people navigate in their daily work life. Symbolic power is both built from and deployed in social interaction. It is through such communication that people jointly cultivate credibility, whether it be during a work task or over a beer at a nearby tavern. It is also through later interactions that this credibility serves as the symbolic power to define "what is happening here," and what is to be done, controlling the actions of others, not with the hammer of authority, but with the comforting blanket of context (Hallett 2007).

Inhabited institutionalism reminds us of the analytic strength of a group focus. Without denying the importance of agency as a general phenomenon, the agency of people (not "individuals") becomes integrated into the agency of the organization within its institutional field. Much external social control is backed by state command or is disputed by oppositional movements that challenge this dominance. Active agents operate in light of institutions, but we can also think of people as exerting *collective* pressure. In the best case, this establishes agreements, often through negotiation, but conflict is also, in its way, collective.

Recognizing power in local communities provides an alternative to portraying institutions as "disembodied structures acting on their own volition while depicting actors as powerless and inert in the face of inexorable social forces" (Colomy 1998: 267). These portrayals have been criticized for their "macrochauvinism," a bias against actors. But we must also avoid "micro-chauvinism" (Turner and Boyns 2002), in which "a sharply defined purposive 'actor'" becomes privileged (Jepperson and Meyer 2011: 57). Microchauvinism elevates individuals as creators of institutional action but downplays both the extra-local social envelope and the power of groups.

If scholars must exhibit bias, we suggest "mesochauvinism." Perhaps we are being overly playful, but for an inhabited institutional approach, the driving force is negotiation in and among groups, producing new routines (Maines 1977; McGinty 2014). By incorporating meaning, action, power, and hierarchy, the inhabited institutional framework balances individual inclinations against the necessity of joint action. Institutional practices merge with interactional orders in establishing systems of constraints.

As a form of local sociology, inhabited institutionalism reveals the value of case studies as an entry point to organizational analysis. Such an approach can lead to a vital comparative analysis that an examination of group cultures across seemingly similar organizations can provide (Fine 1996; Nunn 2014). Inhabited institutionalism demonstrates that institutional pressures shape communal response, but also that the practical implications and meanings of these structural pressures develop from interactions (Binder 2007).

Thinking in Cases

To illustrate the minuet of conflict and control, we begin with an examination of turmoil and change at a Midwestern elementary school. This project ("The Myth Incarnate: Recoupling Processes, Turmoil, and Inhabited Institutions in an Urban Elementary School") developed from two years of observations and interviews by Hallett (2010) with teachers and administrators at "Costen Elementary School," a public K-8 school in a large Midwestern city. The goal of the research was to examine how a new principal, "Mrs. Kox," tried (and failed) to cultivate interactions with the teachers as a means of gaining and using influence to develop accountability. During the ethnography, Hallett observed staff meetings, informal gatherings, classes, and faculty lunches. In addition to focusing on activities within the school, he observed meetings of the local community board. The board, set up by the city education department, attempted to provide parents with some measure of oversight on the operation of the school. What became clear during the research was that conflict over divisive cultures of accountability among communities within the school, coupled with the authority given to or removed from local actors, was central to the turmoil observed.

To understand the process of control, we turn to Fine's ethnographic observation of local offices of the National Weather Service in *Authors of the Storm: Meteorologists and the Culture of Prediction* (Fine 2007). This is a government bureaucracy that produces forecasts at 122 local offices as well as at various specialized sites (such as Severe Storm forecasting, Hurricane modeling offices), and has working groups at the national headquarters outside of Washington, DC. The research was conducted over 18 months, with primary observations and interviews at the Chicago office, watching as the meteorologists created forecasts and dealt with a new computerized system for composing predictions that would be distributed to the public. In addition, comparative research occurred at two other local forecast offices. To gain a deeper insight into the bureaucracy of forecasting, Fine observed at the Storm Prediction Center and with several working groups in the Washington area. The focus was to understand how predictions of the future – attempts at forecasting – were a social and cultural phenomenon that operated in the context of organizational control. How does a bureaucracy work in practice, despite the seeming autonomy given to meteorological scientists? While the central administration gave local offices authority to review data and to serve their community, coordination was necessary among the many locations.

School Daze: Turmoil at Costen Elementary

Hallett's research on the dynamics of turmoil in an urban public elementary school reveals how sustained conflict can produce epistemic distress and the creation of an injustice frame. People matter, and so do their cultures. While conflict can and does occur in larger institutional venues or national spaces, Hallett demonstrates that it may have powerful effects in light of a well-established group culture and interaction order. School employees found that their expectations and routines, tied to images of comfortable past practices, were being upended rapidly and without consent.

Costen School's newly appointed principal, Mrs. Kox, overturned previously accepted and understood local circuits of action that the teachers had created under old rules and which, from their perspective, were successful. As Hallett demonstrates, the new principal desired to create an organization with clear lines of authority and accountability. From the outside, these seem like organizational virtues. However, authority and accountability, at least as instituted, were at odds with the prior local order. Kox hoped to create demonstrable answerability by requiring particular classroom practices and removing a layer of autonomy, but instead produced an ongoing state of conflict. Specifically, she demanded that her teachers focus on measurable and achievable goals, such as an increase in standardized test scores, along with a belief that each classroom should adhere to clear standards of discipline. This ignored the possibility that each teacher might have established a successful classroom culture and interaction order. Kox's policies were tied to an increase in administrative surveillance and bureaucratic paperwork, limiting teacher discretion. However, these demands did not simply constrain individual teachers, but threatened a set of local arrangements as to how the school was to run. It was not simply that particular teachers felt dismayed or aggrieved, but rather that they, as a group, coalesced to protest the changes that seemed to undercut the authority of all.

These new expectations inspired a contrasting set of meanings that provoked continuing conflict between Mrs. Kox and the teachers. Hallett writes of this as constituting a "partisan interpretation," indicating a set of meanings that is locally constituted by interest groups. The division between administrators and teachers provided the grounds for this dispute. This is linked to a meso-level neo-institutional theory that examines the effects of loosely coupled local cultures on the structure of organizations, and also to changes in the interaction order of the school.

Early iterations of neo-institutional theory had emphasized that the development of organizational meaning operates through impression management and interpersonal interaction (Meyer and Rowan 1977: 358). In this case, overstepping established work practices created shared discontent, leading to disruption in the form of what was, in essence, a local social movement.

Opposing these changes, one teacher gathered complaint letters from more than two dozen colleagues that she compiled into a 119-page volume and distributed to central administration. This teacher corralled co-workers into her movement, proudly explaining, "I plastered [Mrs. Kox's] name all over this city. Everybody I could think of I sent that book to. . . . It had, oh God, maybe a good 40 odd letters from various teachers" (Hallett 2010: 65). These teachers treated the organization as their space, valuing their strong group culture and justifying local action to protest what they perceived as injustice. Crucial to Hallett's inhabited institutional approach is that contestation results from how groups perceive threats to their circuits of action. Conflict in institutions results when routines and expectations are disrupted.

This form of conflict constituted "turmoil," a term that was frequently used by the teachers to describe life at the school. Turmoil has two dimensions. First, in response to cultural reordering, teachers shared a sense of epistemic distress: a displacement of meaning, certainty, and expectations (Zuboff 1988: 82). Circuits of action that had guided them in the past no longer applied. Second, they responded to their epistemic distress by (re)constructing a set of meanings that allowed for grievances and defined emergent battle lines.

Before Kox arrived, teachers developed work routines that created a stable set of meanings, knowledge, and expectations. There was loose coordination by grade level, but teachers could develop and use their own teaching practices. Kox's policies disrupted that order, and teachers could no longer operate in accustomed ways. Each day, there was only a limited sense of what might come next. Would Kox observe classrooms? Would she change grading practices? What about the curriculum? Many teachers felt that they were being stripped of the behavioral and cognitive control that organized their occupational world (Weick 1995). One teacher lamented that life became unpredictable because everything "moves from day to day." She struggled with this new "back and forth." Another teacher described her distress in a dramatic fashion. Hands and lips quivering, she explained that she was so "freaked out" by accountability that she brought a trash bag to school, ripping the paperwork Kox used to monitor instruction into "bits and pieces," putting the pieces in the bag, and pouring chocolate milk over it. As one teacher explained, "It has become par for the course not knowing what to expect from day to day." Costen's settled order was in flux. The new principal had created a "problematic present" (Snow et al. 1998) that many found to be psychologically exhausting.

While turmoil is a state of epistemic distress, it has a second component. Epistemic distress involves a collapse of meaning, but collapsed meanings can be built again. Eventually, teachers responded by reconstructing those meanings. Teachers were not just describing their experience of the past but were infusing it with morality. Talk is a basic element in how value is created in the context of group life (Hall 1972; Emerson and Messinger 1977). Even lacking formal authority, staff had informal symbolic power to shape meanings by looking backwards, creating an attachment to their collective memory of a better time (Maines et al. 1983), organizing against the principal's commitment to accountability.

The epistemic distress and emergent partisan battle enveloped Costen in turmoil, affecting everyone at the school. Turmoil is a local outcome, even if it has the potential to spread. But in its situated quality, it provides a means of understanding conflict through a local socio-logical lens. The rules that Kox wished to alter were those that had been embedded in how the faculty at the school saw proper professional practice. Now their culture was being challenged by an outsider, but one with disciplinary authority. Could the group coalesce to preserve what they had treasured? In part they could, as Kox's rules were modified, but eventually both veteran teachers and Mrs. Kox herself exited in the face of test scores that were stubbornly resistant to improvement, despite her demands for accountability. Still, the group culture and the inter-action order were shaken, and circuits of action had to be reestablished.

The turmoil at Costen School is not the only form of conflict; disruption may occur without the presence of such epistemic challenges, and contesting groups may divide with their own traditions. However, in condi-tions of authority and with challenges to that authority, epistemic certainty may be at risk. Hallett's closely observed ethnography of a single school reveals that how morality and meaning are organized in a small group can have profound repercussions.

Storm Clouds of Bureaucratic Control

In contrast to the turmoil at Costen Elementary School, Fine examined forms of control in National Weather Service offices. The forecasters, as individuals and as a team comprising a workplace culture, did not always operate in accord with the National Weather Service's desired policies. They strived for discretion, attacking what they perceived as foolish dictates from above that ignored local conditions. An ongoing tension existed between headquarters and those regional offices that demanded the right to interpret government policy. In other words, the organization of operational meteorology as locally constituted highlighted a tension between independence and control. Technical domains cannot be separated from the organizational infrastructure that they help to create (Sklair 1973). The bureaucrats at headquarters served, in effect, as managers, standing apart from their dispersed staff, but insisting that the public must receive information that bolsters the credibility of the agency and legitimates their assertion of expertise. As purveyors of an integrated public science, they dealt with 122 diverse local cultures.

While every office had a distinct culture, each was embedded in an extended government bureaucracy. The National Weather Service is a branch of the National Oceanic and Atmospheric Administration, itself under the auspices of the Department of Commerce. If these employees claim a scientific mantle, they are also bureaucrats, although few would embrace that label with any enthusiasm. The National Weather Service sets the terms of employment, selects the timing of forecasts, provides the equipment and the data, and publishes lengthy manuals of instruction.

In its culture at headquarters, the weather service is a quasi-military operation. This encouraged a demand for control from above, and the creation of a chain of command. That perspective conflicted with the view in the Chicago office (and other offices) that meteorologists are scientists and should be held to the more informal standards of academic accountability. Cultures were conflicted when policies dealt with dress, informal talk, disputes with other offices, and independence of forecasting choices. With their informality, the forecasters in the Chicago office were treated as a thorn in the side of those who demanded top-down control. This issue was particularly fraught given the errors made by forecasters at the Chicago site when they failed to provide warnings for the deadly 1990 Plainfield tornado. The challenge for the Chicago group was that military structures shaped scientific work.

A structure that focused on the chain of command and accountability to those above rubbed some the wrong way, a culture shock for an agency that had once been managed by academic scientists. One Chicago forecaster persisted in referring to General Kelly, their boss during the Bush administration, as "General Halftrack," after the ineffectual commander in the *Beetle Bailey* comic strip. However, some forecasters elsewhere admired the discipline that the general brought to the agency and his ability to advocate for resources. Under his leadership, the agency was often promoted as a prototype of government accountability. Informants discussed the forms of organizational control from the top with which they had to cope, often with some asperity:

> Certainly now [there is a military tone] . . . . Now we've got the general in charge. . . . It's more of orders, it's more top-down type of thing, and that's not entirely bad. I mean you get things done that way. You can make decisions much quicker. They may be wrong decisions, but you take that risk because you want to move ahead. That's the way the military is. . . . Under the old regime, you studied and studied and maybe you studied it to death. You just took way too long.

* * *

Jerry, an administrator at the National Centers for Environmental Prediction, tells me that he is frustrated with the change in the organization. . . . He suggests that his group is more like a university science department than a military unit. In his group, "people don't like to be told what to do. It's like herding cats."

The debate over control involved distinct models: Is the National Weather Service – and government science in general – academic or military? This debate was played out against the recognition that the weather service is a bureaucracy, which assumes that control derives from a Weberian rationalized structure. Which model best promoted a form of accountability that everyone claims to desire? Control must be systemic, but it is often felt to be absent, in what one forecaster skeptically termed "this multiple tier of incompetence." The issue is not whether critics who decry a lack of accountability are accurate, but, rather, whether the best model is not a university department nor a military unit, but a bureaucracy in which responsibility is diffused to the office as a whole.

Taking a local sociology perspective, we can recognize that debates over the preferred model of structure are not only between headquarters and district offices, but also between individual offices. Two of the sites studied had very different styles of management: the Chicago office and the adjacent "Belvedere" office. As the longer ethnography demonstrates, the Chicago and Belvedere offices operated with dramatically different cultures and authority systems. Chicago was seen, and saw themselves, as skeptical of conformity, independent, and embracing personal autonomy. They modeled themselves on an academic department, wary of dictates from administrators. Joking about the failures of bureaucracy was characteristic of the office, and a forecaster who adhered too closely to the rules of the National Weather Service would be teased or, if unwilling to change, treated with disdain.

In contrast, forecasters in the Belvedere office conceived themselves as organized, controlled, and open to institutional change. The Meteorologist-in-Charge (MiC) prominently posted the accuracy of their forecasts, required by headquarters, whereas in the Chicago office, the report was placed in a back hallway. Either approach can be justified, although the former fits better into the governmental and bureaucratic logic, enabling the office to embrace technological innovation and submit to demands for accountability.

Employees at the Belvedere office, as part of their organizational culture, readily accepted the legitimacy of hierarchy, seeing themselves as integral to the mission of the larger agency. They were led by a meteorologist who continually emphasized lines of authority and accountability. Contrasting himself to his colleague in Chicago, the Belvedere MiC emphasized that he saw himself as a manager. He explained, "I don't want to say I'm a taskmaster. On certain things, I am. . . . I'm probably more of a micro-manager than others. I watch what we produce."

Belvedere staff were willing to trade the recognition that their leader was watching over them for the sense that he was watching out for them. The staff believed that this is how an office should be run. It is not that these meteorologists refrained from griping, but that griping occurred within the context of the *right* of authority to decide. Complaints centered on the content of the decisions, not their legitimacy. In contrast, the Chicago office embraced what might be termed heroic anarchy, a perspective given support by their MiC, who refrained from reining in the actions of his employees. This emphasizes, as local sociology suggests, that how authority and control are enforced and responded to results from the local interaction order and group culture.

Battling Groups

Order is not always orderly, smoothness is not necessarily smooth, and conflict can be creative: these points are important in appreciating the interaction order as it operates in practice. Conflict may be valuable in structuring interaction. This can be recognized if we distinguish between institutions in turmoil and institutions in ferment.

Ferment is not turmoil. A contentious group, organization, or institution can be fulfilling and progressive as the roughness of interaction can force attention to salient concerns, contesting what had once been taken for granted.

How can systems of dispute be managed so that participants feel invested even when their preferred outcomes are rejected? A review of demands for change reveals that groups strive for rights or resources in opposition to other groups that resist the awarding of these benefits. In some cases, a presumption exists that the demands are fully legitimate, perhaps linked to fundamental morality or even natural law. Many once considered slavery to be legitimate servitude, claiming biblical authority. Such a practice now finds no support. This does not mean that current assessments could never change, but such change would be opposed if this well-recognized abomination was newly treated as part of a just social order.

Viewing conflict through the lens of local sociology recognizes that many issues might cause disruption, but what matters is the group process through which actors define, debate, defend, and defy. Moral claims, embedded in local communities, shape the interaction order, as groups with interests and resources demand justice, hoping to gain new adherents and change power relations.

Although various microsociological traditions suggest that the support for smooth and easy interaction is a foundational aspect of social order, this account is incomplete. Rough engagement is crucial in both smaller and wider domains and finds its most powerful home in a world of tiny publics.

Groups are both controlled and agents of control. They are embedded in associations and networks that provide resources and mandates of authority. Organizations, given the extent of their power, may fix relations among groups, and this shapes how workers are constrained. However, we can watch control enacted if we bracket the larger system as a site of legitimation and focus on the dynamics of smaller units, seeing decisions flow from group to group.

Organizations, institutions, and structures are inhabited by people whose ongoing contact creates traditions, rituals, and histories that are used in self-reflexive ways as part of a meaningful idioculture. Models of control invariably emphasize hierarchy: the layering of groups and the lamination of their choices. The right of one community to direct another involves chains of power (Reed 2017): interpretations of legitimate action among groups with differing amounts of influence or resources. We find a cascade of groups, with each dependent on the passage of authority.

While much analysis assumes harmony, groups and their members battle as they face those with rival interests or disruptive intent, both within the group and beyond. To manage, conflict and control are evident. Resource-rich groups, especially those able to channel behavior with the support of state systems, use their power to enforce a vision of moral propriety. Conflict and control belong to local order as much as coordination and civility.

− 7 −
Bridging Groups:
Extending the Local

As they sang, this nondescript and indifferent street audience gazed, held by the peculiarity of such an unimportant-looking family publicly raising its collective voice against the vast skepticism and apathy of life.

Theodore Dreiser, *An American Tragedy*

A focus that rests exclusively on the group as a discrete entity with immediate interaction and intense ties is appealing to those who believe in the power of the local. Yet such an exclusive emphasis ignores how social relations and cultures reverberate throughout society. Only examining knots of communal action, bounded groups, and the strong ties within them misses much. A world exists outside the group, and that world shapes what happens within (Jasper and Volpi 2018).

How, then, can a local sociology engage with this broader, external world? How are groups linked to more extended communities, and what are the implications of those linkages on the meso-level of analysis? More specifically, how do multiple group memberships, networks, and media connect a set of local domains? How do connected groups create "society"?

Exclusive attention to interaction, culture, and social relations is insufficient. While we emphasize the value of treating the group as central to any complete sociology, this view must be balanced with a recognition that a world exists outside the space of any one group. To be persuasive, local sociology must address large-scale organizations, subcultures, media worlds, and online communities.

Action always depends on its setting, but we are more than just local actors. We reside in a complex world. At issue is how a close-knit community is shaped by and shapes worlds outside its boundaries. In this chapter, we engage these concerns. Extended social systems are built from a grid of tiny publics. While larger structures involve a fragmented mesh of small groups, it is never an undifferentiated mass nor a world of isolates.

Extending Local Sociology

Expanding the local sociology perspective to incorporate extra-local conditions recognizes that any group depends upon complex arrangements that exist beyond its boundaries of routine interaction (House 1981; McLeod and Lively 2003). This includes patterns of relations and structures of power. The group, the network, and the organization are inevitably intertwined. Groups serve as tiny organizations within larger ones (Hallett and Ventresca 2006) or as micro-networks (Katz et al. 2004).

Empires – both ancient and modern – and, more recently, the building of metropolises and global systems of governance suggest that expansive political power can overwhelm local control, even when powerful decision-makers constitute a group themselves. Still, as described in chapter 5, widely expansive systems also depend on coordination and collaboration.

The stability of empires – at least for that period in which they are stable – relies on the existence of small groups in the court, military, church, and bureaucracy.

While it might be parsimonious to reduce empires to groups, it would be foolhardy to do so. Authorities have mechanisms for diffusing power. In the course of history, groups establish networks and gather resources to channel and constrain the choices of others. As a result, powerful state systems can limit local governance, bolstering centralized power.

As a historical case, the Roman Empire and its Pax Romana demonstrate the creation of extensive systems of control by means of the power of local outposts. Even more expansive in terms of reach and longevity is the Catholic Church with its headquarters in Rome and its global missions. The structure of the Church of Jesus Christ of Latter-Day Saints or the Church of Scientology suggests that this process is not limited to one theological system or any historical era.

More generally and less dramatically, groups establish first-order ties that may subsequently be bolstered within networks that provide second- and third-order relations: what Nicholas Christakis and James Fowler (2009) speak of as the effect of friends of friends of friends. As a result of this lattice, we desire for our actions to accord with those of others. Even a non-conformist depends on friends. This is crucial to bonding, as described in chapter 5, but when those relations extend beyond our close ties, bridging results.

Whatever the shape of an expansive network, local communities are central nodes with dense ties. Whether influences are direct or indirect, the multiple groups in which actors participate shape their actions. Robin Dunbar's (1993) assertion that the human brain can process 150 associates, if accurate, suggests involvement in a set of smaller communities with cross-group linkages. Bounded groups are linked together through interlocking ties, including multiple group memberships, acquaintance-ships, or exposure to mass and specialized media.

These interlocked structures create the conditions through which an interaction order develops, a world that depends on a complex and differentiated set of social relations. For example, the linkages and shared identities among groups of teens, based on residential ties within local communities, suggest that weak network ties depend on stronger ties to places of action such as gangs, clubs, and teams (Fine and Kleinman 1979). This perspective is likewise evident in Brian Uzzi's (1996) depiction of bonding and bridging ties – both strong and weak – in the fashion industry. While network connections are useful for accessing knowledge and resources, they also protect a community from shocks caused by cultural innovation or changes in membership.

To be effective, group influence must cascade beyond its borders. Just as people have relations, so too do groups, and these relations can be happy or hostile. In chapter 3, we asserted that connections create a feeling of belonging with a world outside of one's close contacts. Within a dense, multi-stranded society, individuals participate in several communities simultaneously (Dowd and Dowd 2003), even if such connections require a complex juggling of schedules (Gibson 2005). Multiple commitments have the potential to produce competing identifications when groups hold distinct values (Wilkins 2008). As described in chapter 2, individuals may value several secondary identities, activated at different moments or integrated within a primary identity.

This leads to appreciating the existence of subcultures as stemming from local sociology. In a complex society, full knowledge of and complete conformity to cultural traditions are rare. Instead, subdivisions create pockets of commitment (Lizardo 2006; Vaisey and Lizardo 2010). Subcultures constitute networks of groups that share a recognizably similar background, focus, or a set of common behaviors. While not necessarily found in a common location, the parallel interests of these communities provide a local sociology with a wider range. When people join together in shared space, such as a park or town square, the subculture as enacted constitutes a scene (Silver, Clark, and Yanez 2010). These gatherings are found in domains as diverse as truffle merchants in Provence (De la Predelle 2006: 139–51), teenage Goths in collegiate America (Wilkins 2008), and poets in Tokugawa Japan (Ikegami 2005: 171–203). What is critical is not that subcultural groups are based on demographic characteristics as such, but that these trans-local scenes trade on broadly known cultural elements (Muggleton 2000).

The possibility of subcultures depends on the diffusion of culture, expanding the reach of traditions. As symbolic interactionist Tamotsu Shibutani (1955: 566) influentially observed, "Culture areas are coterminous with communication channels." In contrast to group-based interaction, subcultures do not rely on co-presence, but rather on the existence of extended lines of communication. While physical places bolster affiliation, virtual sites can also connect face-to-face groups through nodes of dissemination, such as social media or topical discussion boards. These locations establish knowledge forums in which participants trade "culture bits" of which those outside network boundaries are unaware, as with those distinct pools of knowledge that divide racially based public spheres (Maines 1999).

Crucial for spanning knowledge chasms are weak ties that link otherwise distant groups. This bridging is essential if we are to speak of culture beyond the local. These communication channels connect knots of strong relations into a recognizable, but extended, cultural realm. Although we often consider groups as closed systems, participants rarely interact exclusively with one another. A set of *interlocks* or connections that together create the possibility of a "small world" is crucial (Milgram 1967; Watts 1999; Schnettler 2009). Linkages take many forms, but the effect is to share culture beyond an immediate context, extending customs and performances into a more expansive interaction order.

As a result, we must consider how groups intersect. These linkages take many forms and can involve relations among individuals or small groups. In each case, the effect is to create a shared world of discourse and action that becomes a point of reference for each local outpost of culture. The content of subcultures shapes numerous group cultures if content is spread widely. Although interlocks take many forms, we present four: multiple-group membership, structural roles, weak ties, and specialized media diffusion.

Multiple-Group Membership

Few individuals participate only in a single community. More typically, people are involved in several simultaneously, engaging as each group is activated. As a result, people can readily access a wide range of cultural traditions through their overlapping memberships. Take, for example, children at sleepaway summer camp. Not only do camp cabins constitute groups with their own distinctive idiocultures, status hierarchies, and experiences, but each cabin serves as an agora – a trading zone – in which knowledge from the camper's home community is transmitted. Within the camp environment, campers in one cabin know those in others, leading to a culture that is broader than that of any one bunk. When the children return home, these new cultures may be shared, extending their reach (Lanier-Vos 2014). In this way, ideas and practices pass across spatial and temporal boundaries.

Similar processes are found in what Furnari (2014) defines as "interstitial spaces," small-scale settings that host informal, intermittent interactions between people from distant institutional fields, such as hobbyist clubs. These spaces can spawn innovation because people with diverse experiences meet and interact, sharing and expanding their knowledge in the process. A prime example is the "Homebrew Computer Club" in the late 1970s to early 1980s, where enthusiasts from multiple walks of life, ranging from "hippie anti-war activists" to "hard core engineers," who shared a similar leisure interest in computer programming, gathered together, traded ideas, and created the groundwork for what would become Apple computers.

Structural Roles

While participating in multiple groups allows for cultural diffusion, this is particularly applicable to those in favorable structural positions. The person who participates in two ongoing communities with only a few joint members has a crucial position that permits diffusion and cultural change. Individuals who in their work or leisure interact with multiple groups, organizations, or communities can spread information outside tight networks.

While some forms of group participation are bounded, as in the example of the campers discussed above, other roles exhibit greater reach. These include stand-up comics, motivational speakers, and itinerant preachers, who, as part of their performances, spread ideas widely. They have access to multiple audiences that otherwise might have little overlap. Take, for example, the influential, if contentious, comedy of Dave Chappelle, winner of the 2019 Mark Twain Prize. Born and raised in Washington, DC, Chappelle now chooses to live in rural Ohio. By making people laugh, even against their better judgment, he crosses racial divisions, political boundaries, and the urban/rural divide. Although his humor is controversial, the position and the structural role that he fills enables him to share his ideas. In such cases, the primary role obligation of these individuals is not to spread culture from group to group, but diffusion is an indirect result of their multi-group contact. These roles can be powerful given the diversity of those with whom they interact. They are crucial nodes that bridge communities with few other linkages.

Weak Ties

No matter how intense and densely connected their core social relations are, most individuals maintain congenial acquaintanceships outside their primary interacting groups. Networks are rarely fully bounded. Those external contacts or "weak ties" (Granovetter 1973) are crucial for disseminating information. Studies of rumor, gossip, and news in times of stress reveal that information spreads rapidly under favorable conditions: if participants define the information as significant and if the relational structure supports diffusion.

In practice, the weak ties of group members are bounded – associated with racial, class, age, geographic, gender, or religious divisions – that limit these pools of knowledge from being easily accessible to all. Making acquaintances across these boundaries is more challenging than connections with those always present. Yet, "friends" and "followers" on Facebook, Twitter, and Instagram can serve as contacts, and makes their knowledge more accessible.

While weak ties are more likely to cross borders – network gaps or structural holes (Burt 1992) – than are strong ties, boundaries affect the frequency of contact. Further, different networks transmit specialized cultural genres, based on the imagined interest of the target (such as health information, political conspiracies, celebrity gossip, or off-color humor) (Dégh and Vazsonyi 1975). Ultimately, a network depends on the interests and placement of those whose relations influence the culture of groups to which they belong.

Media Diffusion

A final interlock involves specialized media. Media reach numerous groups simultaneously, providing shared knowledge. However, audiences do not access media productions randomly. Consider the distinct audiences for opera, music videos, and jazz festivals. Some listeners have broad tastes, but audiences are not interchangeable. Cultural awareness results from prior interest and this, in turn, shapes the likelihood of future exposure. Research on cultural omnivores (Peterson and Kern 1996) suggests the power and privilege of cultural elites whose tastes tend to be especially wide and resource-rich, appreciating numerous art forms.

We have alluded to the important process of diffusion that takes place online in the Internet's ether. We next turn to the extension of cultures via this broader locale and mediated process. In doing so, we describe the influence of social media and new forms of connection, now so central to how contemporary society is structured.

Tiny Publics in the Cloud

Face-to-face interaction has long been the gold standard of communal life, as well as the focus of analysis for microsociologists. Prior to the COVID-19 lockdowns, and despite the rise of the Internet, it has been how we imagine social relations. However, mediated interactions have become more prominent during the past two decades, and especially recently as a response to restrictions brought on by the pandemic. These technologies simultaneously enable and constrain behaviors, limiting the array of expressions and interpretations available in real life, but also extending interactions beyond physical place and broadening the reach of tiny publics.

Online interactions provide grist for describing the networked communities that exist beyond the boundary of the small group. Can we plausibly speak of these extended worlds of occasional identity as tiny publics? They seem anything but tiny and are often quite vacuous even if they can be viewed as online publics. Still, these broad-based (if algorithm-dependent) relations matter, and local sociology can help to appreciate them. In online communications, when participants in a digital culture are anonymous, hidden by a handle or an avatar, Goffman's (1959) insights about the presentation of self have become more salient, not less so: as back stages are tucked away behind usernames and passwords, the visible presentation becomes all the more "real."

Whether participants are anonymous or known, online communities and interactions have, out of necessity, expanded during the COVID pandemic. Zoom calls permit us to have group chats and keep physical distancing. Of course, these technologically advanced social media are not the only ones that exist outside the spatially proximate world. The earlier existence of a "republic of letters" (Goodman 1994) recognized that written communication creates lines of collaboration that transcend group cultures. Email, in effect, serves as a rapid and insistent postal system, and texting carries some of the immediacy of conversation. Beyond the sociality of the eye, technologies of the ear, such as telephonic equipment, have served much the same purpose (Fischer 1992). Even today, in this era of Zoom, some prefer a phone call as a simpler, if "old-fashioned," means of interaction – a break from sensory overload.

Mediated interactions provide both freedom and constraint. They permit opportunities for resistance, but also allow for layers of surveillance. Like those systems that promise freedom, social media also produce inequality and strengthen power structures. In this, social media are not truly free. For some, the start-up costs of cell phones, computers, and Internet access are prohibitive. Those costs aside, this is evident in the reduced or missed learning opportunities for many students from kindergarten through college in the scramble for online and hybrid learning.

Other power dynamics operate as well. Although online sites encourage interaction, establish membership criteria, and depend on rules of conduct, implicit or explicit, these are often looser, more ambiguous, and less enforced than those found in face-to-face domains. For our argument, they have the potential of creating a range of affiliations that might be unlikely if spatial co-presence is required. However, those who lack access to these media are shut out entirely, and closed virtual doors make their voices unheard (DiMaggio et al. 2001). At times, media can be as much of a barrier as a bridge.

What are the consequences of social media? How does cyberspace permit the development of extended group cultures, even in the absence of face-to-face interaction? Can online and offline communities be integrated, bridging meso-cultures over wide distances? These are broad empirical questions, the topic of many analyses. Perhaps creating an online network of intimate strangers is distinct from face-to-face group dynamics, but there are similarities as well. Online communities are comparatively thin social systems: worlds often characterized by faint local cultures. Nevertheless, as Lance Bennett (2012: 20) argues, new media permit the personalization of politics and, as a result, encourage the gathering of those who embrace similar identities. What appears to be institutional fragmentation and slight relations can at times lead to vibrant dialogue and to the development of new norms, morals, and expectations (Chayko 2008), even if lacking the intimacy of face-to-face interaction.

Mediated channels of experience have bolstered and, in some cases, replaced face-to-face interactions. Direct connections still constitute sensory symphonies, including visual and auditory channels as well as tactile and olfactory ones. In contrast, mediated interactions are more like contained solos. Letters privilege vision, while recognizing that the feel of rich stationery and the smell of a perfumed billet-doux can affect the reader. Telephonic communications privilege the auditory in a setting that, like face-to-face communication, encourages dialogue. Instant messaging and texting blend the visual and the dialogic.

Online spaces are increasingly evident, and local sociology must account for them, but it would be a mistake to overemphasize their influence. For example, despite the attention to popular memes, few messages actually go viral. According to the *Atlantic Monthly* (Meyer 2013), Facebook communities are truly tiny publics: The typical Facebook user has only about 100 friends, and these friends are often linked. Twitter users have an even smaller network: each active user (someone who has tweeted in the past month) has 61 followers, despite the attempts by the company to expand the pool of contacts. In contrast to Facebook, these Tweeters are less likely to follow each other, but they have traits in common. If a user tweets, a small group may respond or may re-tweet.

Although some protests inspired by social media begin with temporary communities with limited interpersonal connections, through the online dispersal of information, identification may emerge if there is a recognition of common values (Courpasson and Dany 2013). Activation through social media does not develop immediately, but because nodes link to other nodes, an extended network is possible. A compelling example is the "no show protest" and disappointing Trump rally in Tulsa in June 2020. In the days and weeks before the rally, a middle-aged woman from Iowa vented her political ire on a TikTok video: "I recommend all of those of us that want to see this 19,000-seat auditorium barely filled or completely empty go reserve tickets now and leave him standing there alone on the stage." Teens across the country and K-Pop fans around the world did just that, reserving thousands of seats and creating the expectation of a full arena and an enormous crowd outside, leading to political embarrassment and concern about the ethics of political pranks (Lorenz, Browning, and Frenkel 2020).

When many local communities are activated simultaneously, a collection of tiny publics can appear to be a mass movement, even if the network involves distinct groupings of friends who only coalesce for an engaging occasion. Given the existence of a diffuse structure, the challenge is to explain how individuals embedded in groups can identify with those beyond the local. Ultimately, the goal is to give online interactions the intimacy that comes with life in a face-to-face world.

Thinking in Cases

Ethnographers recognize that whatever site they select is never entirely contained, even if they narrow their empirical and analytical focus. Walls are always breached. Communities have metaphorical windows and doors. Organizations of hermits are not to be found. In this section, we examine two ethnographies by Fine in light of how these communities are positioned in a wider public: the community of competitive chess, and the world of folk art collectors. While both ethnographies involve the observation of groups, in each case these groups belong to larger fields. Our approach in thinking through these cases embraces what Matthew Desmond (2014) has termed "relational ethnography." An adequate interpretation of society involves seeing how a group is connected to, depends on, and is limited by other groups that are connected to a variety of powerful institutions.

We begin with the chess community, described in Fine's (2015) *Players and Pawns: How Chess Builds Community and Culture*. Chess is a widely known game, both in the United States and globally. It has a well-developed infrastructure, even if it does not receive as much attention as players might prefer. According to some estimates, over 40 million Americans know how to play the game. Ethnographic research on competitive chess took place over five years and involved engagement with a variety of groups and observations at numerous chess tournaments, as well as in-depth interviews with players as diverse as high school students and internationally known grandmasters. Among the core sites of research were the Marshall Chess Club in New York City, a high school team in Chicago, a collegiate chess club in Chicago, a professional team that played in the United States Chess League, and a community-based chess club. Each site had a group with its own idioculture, interaction order, and routine circuits of action. However, that was not all that was involved. The players belonged to a larger social arena. Participants considered themselves connected within a broader leisure world. To understand chess from the local sociology perspective, we examine meaningful connections, returning to issues of collective identity.

Next, we examine a four-year study of self-taught art, *Everyday Genius: Self-Taught Art and the Culture of Authenticity* (Fine 2004). This covers a genre that is occasionally referred to as folk art, outsider art, or vernacular art. The choice of label has implications for how the field is perceived and how individuals within it engage with each other. The creators of these works stand outside the world of trained and institutionally embedded artists. While the primary focus of this project centered on collectors, it also involved relational ethnography, incorporating dealers, critics, curators, and the artists themselves. The intersection of these groups was the core of the analysis.

In contrast to other ethnographies discussed in this book, there was no central meeting place. As a result, fieldwork at organized road trips, shows, art fairs, auctions, and lectures bolstered data collected through interviews. Observations also took place at meetings of Intuit: The Center for Outsider and Intuitive Art, located in Chicago. During the course of the observations, close ties developed with many prominent actors in each role. However, in contrast to the research on Little League teams or meteorological offices, the focus was not on the development of a singular group culture.

Over the Board

Chess is an activity that is played in many locations under diverse conditions. Many parents teach their children the rudiments of the game and see this as part of building their offspring's cultural capital. Or two chums may break out a board simply for a friendly contest. In these examples, chess does not intersect with a broader community. As a game, chess requires only two persons, perhaps with an uncertain understanding of the rules and possibly with different levels of interest. In its simple form, play requires little in the way of commitment.

However, as a subculture, chess demands more. Here the activity must acquire meaning within an extended community to produce identification that transcends the local. In this world, one does not merely play chess, but, rather, one *is* a chess player. The chess subculture requires an infrastructure that is both cultural and physical. Chess is society as well as play. It constitutes a soft community: a social scene that is potentially open to anyone as long as they demonstrate a desire to join and to follow the rules of the game. The embrace of chess is sufficient for entry. Personal eccentricities, unless extreme, are discounted. These men and women are part of the community, even though that scene is divided by status, skill, and background, including age, ethnicity, and gender.

In the world of chess, showing commitment is sufficient for acceptance. This commitment creates an ongoing connection with the activity and its denizens. Players engage in the group and in the world; they prioritize identities that are crucial. For Pierre Bourdieu (1996: 227–8), this constitutes *illusio*, an investment in a social world that is of *interest* for participants. The chess player who persuades his wife that he must attend the club every Thursday reveals his priorities. So does the person who pays dues to the United States Chess Federation, joins a high school team, takes lessons from a master, spends a weekend at an out-of-town tournament, or hunches over a computer competing against those a continent away. Each of these reminds us of the limits of a narrow group focus. In addition, some chess players use their skills to engage in competitive poker or bridge, linking leisure worlds.

We find the bridging role of chess most clearly in arranged tournaments: some are scholastic, designed for children; others are for seniors; some are strictly local; some are national or regional, called Opens, and accessible to anyone with the entrance fee; others are Invitationals; and a few highly select tournaments are for global grandmasters. We see these locales in the popular mini-series *The Queen's Gambit*. The large or important ones are sponsored by longstanding organizations, such as the US Chess Federation or the World Chess Federation. Considering the range of tournaments, we can map an archipelago of chess, but also, given connections and the ability to play in several types of tournaments, bridges between islands. These contests are crucial for maintaining chess as a vital social world. The range of tournaments is central to the networking of the chess community.

The vitality of competitive chess depends on a flowering of tournaments, bolstering its emotional and financial economy and knitting the activity together, despite the widely diverse spaces in which games are played. Tournaments can celebrate community, both in gathering people and in sharing activity. Players suggested that, when successful, tournaments "have a warm feel to them, a very rich and pleasing experience." Despite being embedded in local groups, competitors desired a broader community. One player spoke of the World Open in glowing terms: "I love going to those tournaments. All of the most ardent players are put into one room to compete. It is kind of like the Super Bowl. Everyone who loves the game and the best players are there. Everyone is there for chess, and it is so much more intense." While not every player would be as enthusiastic as this strong competitor, he recognized how communal a tournament can be. These events are festive spaces for ingathering and for making connections. A tournament organizer suggested the multiple functions of the National Open. He explained that a successful tournament must attract players, distribute rewards (monetary prizes in adult tournaments and trophies in scholastic ones), function smoothly, and be fun, while creating a time for socializing. Set times and spaces allowed these soft communities to be integrated in a large convention hall, hotel ballroom, or library community room. Through the efforts of entrepreneurs, these events provided individuals and friendship groups with emotionally charged, networked occasions. The institution of the tournament suggested that games matter, and this *mattering* drew attendance. Whenever members of a group or a subculture can persuade others that they are doing something that is vital, commitment rises. If chess is not merely a child's game but a link to cognitive development or to Western cultural history, participants will come to believe that they are engaged in something more profound than meaningless play.

Tournaments, in their diversity, revealed the multiple places of the chess world. Like many voluntary domains, chess is a community of communities, a space where diverse groups overlap (or choose to ignore each other). Players delighted in attending tournaments, despite losing records. A handful of participants received prizes and won enough cash to cover their expenses. For a very few, chess is a livelihood, or at least contributes to a livelihood. This much smaller group was important for the chess community because of the aspirations that it provides for others. Publicity about these leading figures occasionally reached those outside the world of chess, establishing an extended community, as in the case of Bobby Fischer's Chess Boom in 1972 or that of *The Queen's Gambit* more recently.

Virtually all competitors, even chess champions, held a day job, have benefitted from a trust fund, or could persist thanks to an employed spouse. In the gendered world of competitive chess where men still dominate, employed spouses were most likely to be women who indulged their husbands. As one chess organizer reported,

> Some of the top grandmasters are married to women who have very good jobs so they can travel around the country and the women allow them to have this occupation as a professional chess player. Like Grandmaster A's wife is a surgeon, Grandmaster B's

wife is an attorney, Grandmaster C's wife is a computer programmer. So, by these women having these high-powered jobs, it keeps the family going so their husbands can go around the country and play chess.

To be a "chess professional" doesn't mean you earn enough to support a family or even have financial independence. Perhaps for these reasons, being a "chess professional" was once stigmatized, even a mark of shame, but today top players – as in the worlds of bridge or poker – are honored celebrities, at least within the community.

How many people earn a significant portion of their livelihood from competitive chess? Because of the diversity of chess, it is hard to know, aside from realizing that the number is very small in contrast to the 40-plus million Americans who know how to play the game. There are players in Washington Square Park in Greenwich Village, who are part of the "underground economy" and are condescendingly termed "hustlers." This subworld occasionally receives media attention and attracts tourists. These men, pleasing novices and thrill-seekers, have some of the air of carnival barkers. One man kept repeating, "Chess players. Come on over. No gambling. No clock." This mantra slid into a financial transaction, either through betting or by direct payment. Many games were a three-minute blitz, spiced with trash talk, an exciting scene (Waitzkin 1988: 17–25). This community, once primarily Jewish, is now largely Black and Latino. Although they have only a loose, casual, and occasional overlap with scholastic and tournament play, these men are treated as a vital and stimulating part of the chess world.

Beyond this vivid subculture are those who hope to use chess for "legitimate" employment. One New Yorker, familiar with chess scenes, estimated that fewer than 100 Americans earn their living exclusively from playing or writing about chess. When one adds teachers, tournament organizers, or those who sell chess equipment, the number might reach several thousand. With the expansion of scholastic and high school chess, teaching has become a growth area, even if it is not highly lucrative. However, top teachers earned a comfortable living from teaching, both face-to-face and through online training, charging at least $200/hour to parents of promising students (Hoffman 2007: 60). These instructors depended on a global circuit of chess, especially beneficial to Russian émigrés. Given the overlap of those involved, the world of elementary school chess has increasingly become tied to elite tournament chess, an impressive example of how diverse communities can be merged.

At the pinnacle of chess, top players have achieved some measure of financial stability, aided by writings and endorsements. With the exception of a very few, such as Garry Kasparov, income derives from the community. During the Cold War, the Soviets supported their champions in the style in which other members of their elites were treated. Such was not the case in the capitalist United States where top players, even Bobby Fischer, had to scrape by and push for larger tournament prizes (Cockburn 1974: 129). Today, given the disposable income of many amateur players who are professionals in other fields, some top players command a $25,000 appearance fee. As Kasparov said of one championship, "[America] is the centre of the financial world. If you want to succeed as a professional sport you must be in America. . . . This is where the money is. . . . You could see it on CNN International. That changed the rules of the game. We are a legitimate professional sport now" (Geuzendam 2006: 53–4). With his gold Audemars-Piguet wristwatch, Moscow apartments, and bespoke suits, Kasparov embodied the financial possibilities for celebrity players.

What became clear is that chess is not a world – a single community – but, rather, a set of intersecting worlds, linked by occasional connections. With the presence of online platforms that allow for speed chess or blitz among players from around the globe, a game that was once localized has broken wide open, welcoming a broad range of players. Chess could once be spoken of as an over-the-board activity of a community chess club, a high school team, a gentlemen's club, or a set of friends who have a weekly chess night. However, to understand chess today is to recognize that, while groups still provide anchors, tournaments and Internet play provide sails through which movement in this social sea is possible.

The Artist and the World

In playing chess, all participants do essentially the same thing, despite their diversity: they play chess – admittedly in different settings, with different styles, and with vastly different ability. Now we turn to our second case, one with widely disparate roles: that of self-taught art. We move from the analysis of a subculture to that of a scattered domain with a recognizable, if occasionally blurry, division of labor. An ethnography that focused only on the artist would provide a truncated and incomplete picture. The world of self-taught art depends on a tapestry of diverse actors, groups, and organizations. This is true for many reasons, especially since most outsider artists are barely connected to – and even largely unaware of – the institutionalized art world. The community of those who are involved with self-taught art can be spoken of as constituting a relational community, a domain of intersecting fields. The "world" of self-taught art – no matter the number of groups – represents a focused network bound by shared interest and revealing a diversity of roles.

This field consists of collectors, dealers, critics, academics, curators, and museum professionals (possibly including a rare artist). Occasions are set for these actors to meet. Along with the annual meeting of the Folk Art Society of America, shows, such as the Outsider Art Fair in New York or Folk Fest in Atlanta, permitted the gathering of members of the community beyond their local worlds. On these occasions, a transactional market became a space of friendship, and network gossip and shared festivity revealed the belonging and the bonding that people shared. Gallery open houses, museum openings, occasional symposia, and auctions also allowed for friends and associates to reconnect.

Consider, for example, the "Finster Fest," named after the Revd. Howard Finster, a prominent Georgia self-taught artist, and held in 2000 after he had been released from the hospital with double pneumonia. The self-taught art community gathered to pay tribute to this beloved artist in the sunset of his life. Emotions were evident and mixed, a moment of somber joy as Revd. Finster gave what many imagined might be his final sermon and signed autographs. Dealers, collectors, critics, filmmakers, and fellow artists were present, as were neighbors and family members. Their attendance revealed the extent and commitment of the folk art community.

At bridging events such as festivals, shows, parties, and auctions, giddy excitement was common. The first night of the Outsider Art Fair had this quality. This opening reception – a fund-raiser for the American Folk Art Museum – permitted collectors the first opportunity to examine the dealers' wares. However, it was more than this. Long-time attendees, many from out of town, emphasized that, for them, it was a social event at which they knew "everybody." For the moment, self-taught art was a wispy community, a gathering of curators, dealers, collectors, and a few carefully invited artists. The event bridged a community that otherwise existed by phone or online. This world included those who shared interests and values but had different roles.

In addition to public events, open to anyone with the requisite entry fee, other bridging events were by invitation. Each year at the Outsider Art Fair, galleries held dinners or arranged parties for good friends and potential customers, extending the field. Occasionally, salons or seminars linked the diverse community. Parties held by Greenfield Village museum director Robert Bishop became legendary. As recounted by Julia Ardery (1998: 206–7):

> Bob [Bishop] in the early seventies, started having what you might call folk art "salons" over at his house. They were actually just the funniest cocktail parties you ever saw in your life because Bob could put together the strangest menagerie of friends you can imagine for a party. He was comfortable across all sorts of class lines. . . . And the guest list would include very sedate, conservative . . . "old wrinkled money" collectors from Birmingham, Michigan, and Grosse Point who would find themselves rubbing shoulders with very stuffy curators from the Henry Ford Museum who in turn would be rubbing shoulders with college students and young collectors from Cranbrook. All these folks were thrown in with businessmen, art investors, and sometimes even motorcycle club members, all of whom would find themselves discussing Bob's latest finds with people in green chiffon cocktail dresses and beehive hairdos that Bob had met at some seminar on quilts that he had run over at the museum. . . . *He also was building, very carefully, a new coalition of people who might be interested in American decorative and folk arts.* [Emphasis added]

In any social world, certain individuals serve – as did Robert Bishop – as connectors, bridging the disparate segments of a social world that might not overlap, expanding it outward. Bishop's soirées reflected a crucial technique of extension, as each guest was part of their own group. In effect, Bishop created a network of groups that might not otherwise have existed.

Once developed, latent networks can be activated as needed. We see this in the case of artists who face life crises or need post-mortem support. In one such instance, art collectors and dealers gathered – after the fact – to purchase a grave marker for Sister Gertrude Morgan. Prominent Louisiana self-taught art enthusiasts assembled for a moving dedication ceremony, along with the Preservation Hall Jazz Band.

In considering social circles, we often assign people to particular roles. However, what was clear in the self-taught art scene was that the assignment to a single slot is misleading. Groups are open to multiple forms of engagement. Participants may accept several roles – either sequentially or simultaneously – and these roles bolster each other. One informant explained that, in this world, there is the artist, the collector, the curator, the dealer, and the critic, but these are not necessarily different persons. Julia Ardery (1998: 223–4) (herself a critic and an academic) wrote that "dealers routinely wrote catalog essays touting the artists whose works they had for sale and collectors . . . authored picture books featuring their own possessions." Call it synergy, call it hypocrisy. Multiple and permeable roles frequently extend and connect developing fields.

This and other cases compel us to rethink the assumption that individuals are necessarily assigned to distinct roles. As groups become fields, roles overlap, and this overlap allows for an extended community. We recognize this when referring to clearly separate domains (parent, daughter, gallerist, chess grandmaster), but these multiple roles can coexist, and intersections are important for creating bridges that connect subworlds. This becomes easier when, as in the case of social media, communication becomes more fluid and less costly.

A dealer who is also a collector must choose what to present, the artist is motivated by the choices that must be made if also selling the work directly, the critic's remarks may be colored by what is to be placed at auction, and the academic is tempted to supplement a salary by curating the works of favored artists. Conflicts of interest abound, but perhaps this is natural when people do not wish to be confined to a single category of activity. The case of self-taught art, in its divisions and in its complexities, reveals how roles knit groups and spaces of activity. Both chess and art worlds demonstrate that simply observing a face-to-face group is insufficient for understanding the complexity of social relations that exist in a wider relational field.

Bridging Groups

Despite our emphasis on the local, if we exclude larger communities, the perspective will mislead. Groups may be the kernels of society, but they matter because of how they are extended. The recognition of patterns of connections permits us to appreciate what happens in deep and dense worlds. Tiny publics, while rarely absent, are often tied to networks and institutions with access to vast resources. Although expansive institutions depend on groups to mobilize actors, organizations gain influence because people and their tiny publics agree that these larger entities matter. Few groups, however intense their interaction, can withstand the resource control of those with more power. Although authoritarian governments require committees, departments, and boards, local communities rarely meet these dominant actors directly, apart from their media representations. The presence of "government" typically takes the form of downstream enforcers, such as police squads, bureaucratic offices, and those who belong to a street-level bureaucracy (Lipsky 2010). This applies even in societies in which the state hopes to be protective, not oppressive.

Recognizing that the world is divided and contentious, those who engage in extension work by moving local concerns into a broader civic sphere must realize that barriers will have to be overcome. Alliances are needed; connections are essential among tiny publics, and sometimes those pathways are tightly guarded. The logics of community must appeal to a wider network, and this can happen as members of one group perform in venues in which others are audiences. Online communication aids this process of extension as open discursive spaces permit the transcending of the local.

Media could not exist without small groups that produce and distribute content, but, in contrast to face-to-face interaction, content can readily reach large numbers of viewers and listeners simultaneously. Not all these audiences are groups, as individuals can consume media in isolation, but reports of what was seen or heard in the media are often treated as legitimate topics. Whether the audience is composed of individuals or groups, media potentially create collective memory. However wide the network, it establishes shared awareness for each tiny public. Media organizations begin with sets of creators and then, as content is distributed and consumed, they shape the responses of audiences, often tiny ones.

Our argument throughout this chapter, in considering subcultures, networks, social media, and more established media, is that a singular focus on the moment of interaction and the relations among individuals is insufficient. While we emphasize the importance of treating the local level of analysis as central to a fully developed sociology, this view must be enriched with a recognition that the world exists outside the walls, the windows, and the gates of any one community. Action always depends on a limited stage, but we are more than just local actors. We perform in a large theater in which many may attend.

− 8 −

Better Sociology:
A Call to Small Arms

Life is so unlike theory.

Anthony Trollope

To assert that groups constitute the heart of social life and must be central to sociological analysis might be seen as an act of theoretical hubris. No one level of analysis should be privileged. And, in truth, we do not go quite so far. Individuals can hang together without ever becoming groups, and institutions build structures in which close-knit communities are not essential. Some opportunities and constraints are not local in their operation, and local sociology is not all of the discipline.

Nevertheless, the case that we make is a call to small arms − not to ignore far-reaching forces or to dismiss individual heroes, but to emphasize local sources of power. We hope that this volume will allow readers to critique and then embrace a model of social life that treats ongoing interaction as essential. Groups are the crucible where action occurs. Recognizing the primacy of a sociable world is essential to understanding society. It is not that all sociologists must incorporate groups into their research, but this level of analysis should not be ignored. Theory advances through a robust localist focus: a world of tiny publics. Without such an emphasis, sociology is a thin discipline. Sociology must embrace *sociality*. Local sociology is but one label that could describe our argument, a perspective that emphasizes *ongoing relations*, *shared memories*, *common places*, and *collaborative action*. Interaction is consequential because it shapes people's understanding of the past, present, and future, as well as recognizing a here and a there. The emphasis on the temporal continuity of interaction and its spatial embeddedness has not always been made as forcefully as it should be. This is our charge.

However, we do not believe that interaction alone – interaction separated from the recognition of routine social practices – is sufficient. We do not advocate a purely micro-level vision. Instead, we emphasize the meso-level: the intersection of action and structure. We build this argument from numerous disciplinary traditions, notably those of Georg Simmel and George Herbert Mead, but with recognition of the insights of Max Weber and Émile Durkheim as well. Every historian of sociology recognizes that the classical theorists did not depend on a single level of analysis but presented a full-scope discipline. These scholars recognized personal choice, structural constraints, and communal sensibility. While we focus on the last, we do not deny the others. We conceive of the group as a *crucible* in which action takes place, and as a *hinge* that connects the other levels, creating a semi-autonomous linkage of agency and structure. This both encourages and constrains free will in response to the actions of others.

In developing our approach, we draw on sociological research and the theory of group life. This has been a part of sociology even if our colleagues have not always explicitly recognized this focus as a distinctive level of analysis. It is through groups, cementing individuals into ongoing, self-reflexive projects, that community is built. Describing tiny publics is part of our disciplinary birthright, in that groups address emplaced, embodied, historicized, and structural forms of sociability. Local sociology recognizes that ongoing interactions bind people and connect them to institutions through the continuity of personal relations. A social order in which individuals do not maintain routine contact, or where they do not consider that contact to be salient, is a weak domain. Without the power and the potential of community, resilience is impossible. The adjustments that negotiation and flexibility provide are central to any strong system of relations.

In this conclusion, we restate our argument, both in general terms and in light of the specific concepts that were raised in the previous chapters. What does it mean to be a local sociologist? Our model provides a set of building blocks – seven premises for a local sociology:

1. Local sociology takes sociality, group consciousness, and interpersonal relations as crucial to both individual agency and the organizing practices of institutions. It demands a commitment to understanding social order not as a feature of individuals or of institutions, but as a feature of tight-knit communities.
2. It is through group life that people have recognizable selves. Identity construction begins with an expression of sociality. As a result, local sociology depends on an understanding of the identities that being a part of a group provides.
3. Local sociology requires an understanding of feelings of belonging to a community. Belonging operates through an enshrinement of social relations, a central feature of local sociology. Tight engagement creates the conditions for coordination to achieve shared goals, promoting the development of connections and social capital that help those who are a part of the group to extend their opportunities.
4. Culture, as a form of practice and as a negotiated order, belongs to the meso-level of analysis. The group focus compels us to specify the content and the boundaries of cultures and to recognize that groups themselves

depend on shared practices. Cultures mediate between environment and action, enabling us to identify the process by which meaning is created.

5. The small group is a means through which people commit to communities and institutions, motivating them to act in ways that they might not do without interpersonal support. When actions engage individuals within civil society, these groups become tiny publics and are the basis through which societies address collective problems.

6. Conflict and control belong to local order as much as coordination and civility. Disputes may emerge from interaction, and, in turn, recognized, patterned conflicts structure interaction. Disruption precipitates change, challenges inequality and oppression, and can rearrange taken-for-granted assumptions.

7. Groups are connected to, depend on, and are limited by others. These are often connected to a range of institutions. Extending local sociology to consider extra-local conditions suggests that a group operates within complex arrangements that exist beyond the boundaries of routine interaction.

These seven premises emphasize that human life is group life, a reality that defines our humanity and reveals the centrality of interaction orders for any social science that hopes to explain the world as lived.

In the pages that follow we elaborate these premises, stressing that local sociology privileges neither individuals nor institutions, but rather the interacting groups in-between. It is through group life that people acquire a sense of self, and it is through these webs of activity that social structures are continually reproduced and are, at times, remade. For predictable interaction, culture, identification, common spaces, and recognized relations are necessary. Even if we struggle to specify how groups differ from networks, communities, and organizations, the existence of connections defines the social world.

Together, a web of groups establishes meaningful linkages that have both retrospective and prospective qualities. They are not mere structures or patterns, but rather are communities of interaction. Any sociology that ignores the salience of action is hardly sociology at all.

As we noted in chapter 1, it is not simply that microsociology provides a foundation for macrosociology, or that macrosociology provides a foundation for microsociology, but that interacting groups are the meso-cement that binds them together. Local context, as seen through group action, connects structure and interaction through culture. However, on its own, interaction lacks a framework through which action creates stability, and it also lacks a means of generating collective identity. The solidity of communities addresses these absences. Even when scholars accept the reality of structural conditions and the effects of immediate interaction, we must face the challenge of explaining the process by which agentic choices fit within an obdurate and material reality. Group cultures organize action into systems of constraints and opportunities, channeling what is seen as legitimate and even possible. Participants recognize these limits and opportunities, even if sociologists have, at times, been loath to do so.

Groups are also tied to spaces, and that permits us to understand how groups and society are mutually constituted. This is why we refer to spaces as places; the wording transforms the physicality of space into the meaningfulness of place (Gieryn 2018). The salience of scenes in supporting communal culture generates a continuity of belonging. At times, groups are explicit in their criteria of membership, but on other occasions these criteria are vague. Here, we find a world of near-groups, quasi-groups, meet-ups, hang-outs, weak ties, and social happenstance. Although some measure of shared identity is essential, the formality of allegiance varies widely.

A group need not have a formal structure and regular meetings. Rather, it can express an idea of sociality that can be activated or not as the occasion demands. This is particularly salient as people can participate in several groups simultaneously and develop distinct identities from their involvement with each. Few people are only active in a single social domain. Still, however formulated, these linkages operate not only on the cognitive or emotional level, but also by recognizing that identity claims are expressed in action, cementing people to scenes, creating boundaries with other scenes, and recognizing the bridges that connect them.

Community depends upon the benefits that local cultures provide, both to individuals and to larger units, as evidenced in social relations, material resources, and collective action. Further, groups are connected through networks and these relations, even if not explicit sources of support, may provide desired resource exchanges. While groups and networks are not synonymous, groups essentially constitute nodes: areas of the network in which social relations are dense, strong, and meaningful. Structure, as we define it, constitutes an integrated web of social worlds with associated local cultures. Intersecting groups and the forces that bind them, often to other groups with surveillance and resource power, provide the basis on which structure operates. Ultimately, society is a remarkable achievement by people who work jointly, and this justifies Erving Goffman's concept of an inter-action order as a system that depends on interpretations of structures.

As noted, participants routinely engage in multiple worlds, both simultaneously and sequentially, and, as a result, they become aware of other domains that provide models for action: this enables a comparison of social contexts. Integrated groups form institutions, commu-nities, and societies that, although grounded in local scenes, are larger, more established, and more solid.

However, groups do not only coalesce; they also have the potential to fragment and stratify and to establish rivalry. Through the choices of individuals to engage, and through the recruitment of participants, groups build, strengthen, and reproduce divisions. Few communities welcome all, and frequently they replicate exclusive relations and privileged cultures. Entry points are micro-political boundaries that reinforce differentiation and structural discrimination when there are understandings of who is welcome to join and who is not. The acceptance of local citizenship can be fraught. The decision as to which applicants can participate in action scenes determines the fate of local cultures and, as a result, wider publics.

While embracing the value of a meso-level analysis, we admit its limits. To focus solely on the local downplays the isomorphic qualities of social relations and potentially diminishes the recognition of webs of power. While small groups may develop military policy or tax rates or media productions, large populations (armies, voters, home owners, or consumers) have considerable impact in ways that are not easily found in small communities. To erase structures of authority or the influence of market economies as they are given and as they are taken is to present a truncated worldview that ignores the impact of the decisions of powerful entities that are often treated as incapable of being challenged. And yet, erasing the agentic choices of actors to withhold support, to reject consensus, or to contest what others have established minimizes the potential clout of those who can draw on the resources that their backgrounds provide.

How are institutions and webs of power built, if not through groups? One would be hard pressed to find a case in which such structures are developed in the absence of minute associations. These frameworks are real, and people feel their effects. Nonetheless, their behavioral basis may be ignored if the relations among groups are treated as standing above the level of action. This recognition of how interaction slides into structure is crucial for any sociological perspective. Explaining how this happens within an interaction order is, as Erving Goffman (1983: 17) reminded us, our sociological inheritance and what we can bequeath.

The Six "Bs" of Localism

Having laid out a broad theory of localism, we turn to those important concepts that constitute it – what could be called the "six 'Bs' of localism": being (identity), belonging (commitment), building (idioculture), bonding (cohesion), battling (conflict), and bridging (networks). Each chapter, with its empirical grounding in two ethnographic cases, provides a lens through which we watch local communities at work. By moving from the individual to the social system, we ask how groups shape individual identity, and how individuals give groups tensile strength through their desire for commitment.

In discussing shared identities in the chapter "Being in Groups," we describe the linkage of the self with the social. We start with the person. These are people who are defining themselves not as unique beings, but as a part of communities. This corresponds to the looking-glass self as explained by Charles Horton Cooley, while considering the existence of groups and communities that are seen through that looking-glass. While selves are shaped by individual propensities and the limits of human psychobiology, there is also a sociology of self-definition that depends on where one is located and with whom one communicates. When we ask, "Who are you?," the answers celebrate those groups and social categories that matter.

Identity is not merely a personal designation, nor is it automatically provided by one's place within a social structure: it is tied to affiliation with, and participation in, groups. This view takes into account that the choice of which groups matter is shaped by whom one conceives oneself to be, given one's experience, and where in the social structure one desires to be located, given the cartography of communities. Any model of identity formation and embracement that does not incorporate how these models of the self are located is incomplete.

Identity is crucial to individuals, but identities become salient and sticky by virtue of being a part of a tiny public. This is the focus of the next chapter and the next step in creating a local sociology. In "Belonging to Groups," we emphasize the importance and development of commitment. While people may participate for a host of reasons, what impels them to *remain* in those groups? The answer is that they develop a feeling of belonging. Indeed, in all of the ethnographic projects described in this volume, this attachment is crucial. Once participants in social circles become regulars, they are more than just tourists; they are residents of an engaged community. Groups could not exist and could not be stable without the connection between self and others as linked through a desire to belong.

In the first pair of chapters, we examined the individual in groups. Then we turned to groups as locations in which people act together, treating them as spaces in themselves. In an important sense, the corresponding pair of chapters – "Building Groups" and "Bonding by Groups" – are the heart and soul of a local sociology, emphasizing the locality and the community as places of meaning.

"Building Groups" emphasizes what might be the most central concept of local sociology: the role of shared culture or idioculture in channeling behavior. Group involvement depends on the reality that participants will recognize the contours of these meanings, even if not everyone knows all things, and admitting that what constitutes the culture can be ambiguous at times. That culture, including traditions and collective memories, provides the basis through which participants recognize that they have a shared past and a set of common references. Content matters and characterizes the interaction order.

Local cultures are linked to interaction scenes. This focus provides a visible grounding, and with it culture becomes recognizable, instead of being an indescribable mist. Meaning is always linked to action, and action is always connected to social relations. In this sense, a shared ethos makes groups unique, specific, and stable. While all of the ethnographies presented are accounts of how communities develop culture, the studies of baseball teams and gaming groups are explicit in demonstrating how shared cultural elements foster the ability to work together. "Bonding by Groups," as described in chapter 5, reminds us that Alexis de Tocqueville's minute communities are central to collective action. Collaboration begins with the commitment described previously but expands through the necessity of individuals working together. Collective action has long been a basis of sociological analysis, but it is not something that just happens casually. Analyses of social movements have attempted – often with considerable success – to explain the conditions that lead individuals to collaborate. Going further, we argue that collective action begins with the need to bond, rather than through pressures of external resources or the psychology of stress. The belief that members of a community have a shared fate and a common vision permits colleagues to pull together. However, the presence of joint activity does not assure that the goals are broadly desirable. In other words, collective action may produce destructive outcomes, not serving the interest of other groups or even that of each member.

Sociologists properly emphasize these political implications. Yet it is often the case that, as in our empirical examples, this engagement may only involve issues about which influential members of the group care. In any case, it is coordination that matters, and bonding permits the organization of what Herbert Blumer (1969) described as the linking of lines of collective action.

The final pair of chapters demonstrate how local sociology extends beyond the boundary of any particular group. While interaction orders and group cultures are important, a proper sociology requires that forces located beyond the boundaries of the group be considered. Every sociological approach must consider institutions, organizations, and non-interactional forms of structure, even when asserting that local cultures set the conditions for larger effects.

In examining "Battling Groups," we address challenges to civil respect. The emphasis on coordination and shared cultures in much of the book, while important, has limits. Local sociology does not claim that all is sunny and bright. Instead, forces of control and conflict shape group life. Further, disruption need not be treated as a simple destructive force; conflict can at times be heroic. Conflict can be challenging, but local sociology distinguishes between "disruptions for" and "disruption of." The former, having a goal of producing positive social change, can build cohesion. The latter can tear groups apart.

Likewise, while extreme forms of control are oppressive, this use of power is often a reality within and across groups. As groups abut each other, one group may have the authority to decide, and to use its resources to shape and constrain the decisions of other groups with less power and fewer resources. Even though this removes some authority from those with fewer resources, it constitutes an established social order. Recognizing a hierarchy of tiny publics is a way to conceptualize institutional structures. Power does not magically appear from above, but groups are found all the way up and all the way down, each making decisions that enforce its own view of civility and propriety. Publics with fewer resources may – and often do – treat these forms of power and resource control as being entirely legitimate, while those elsewhere see some of these enforcements as dysfunctional, or worse.

Chapter 7, "Bridging Groups," attempts to infuse local sociology with an extra-local transcendence. Society is constituted by a lattice of publics. This permits us to escape the limits of an interaction regime and see the power of subcultures, traditional media, and social media. We emphasize that sociology must recognize the realm of the global. The COVID-19 virus provides a sharp reminder that, however much we wish to treat groups as constituting the basis of order and of meaning construction, obdurate realities cannot be denied. The spread of a global virus inevitably depends on interpersonal connections, even if the persons are not in verbal communication or physical touch but are only linked by a sneeze or a cough.

The metaphor of group cultures as isolated islands is incomplete, because there are bridges that link publics. The bridges are as important as the islands for understanding how communication has influence and how meanings spread. Despite our desire to promote a meso-level analysis – a perspective that deserves more attention and that will pay large dividends – we recognize that, for many sociologists, the focus on bridging local worlds is essential and, without it, local sociology would be incomplete.

A Local Sociology

We reach the end of our text, hoping that we have been neither too harsh nor too narrow. We chose to write this monograph to explain the basics of our local sociology approach in a way that is suitable for both the student and the interested scholarly reader. In so doing, we argue that sociology has not paid sufficient attention to groups, to shared spaces, and to collective action.

Group life provides a basis by which individuals fit into society, and through which social structures shape the contours of action. This is our strong belief, the basis of our research, and our central argument. The group establishes and validates meanings that constitute how people identify themselves, that they belong, that they can work together, that they share meanings, that their conflict and control are worth fighting over, and that they are not isolated. Those groups to which we belong are communities, often with boundaries and divisions, and within them inequalities may be resisted or reproduced.

The existence of cohesive publics does not presume the absence of inequalities, prejudices, biases, or cultural divides. Groups embrace, expand, fracture, and clash, both internally and within the wider social system. Their salience challenges sociologists to expand our models, open our methods, and enlarge our theories.

While we have relied on our field investigations – a means of seeing people at work and at play – there are many ways of describing the meso-level: experimentally, historically, through interviews, or by surveys. But, for us, the ethnographic eye and the observational ear account for people doing things together and justify our approach.

But whichever methodology is chosen, we require a vision to discover society – perhaps a subculture, a social world, or even a scene. In these cases, we find people who are, along with others, committed to their histories, their relations, and their spaces. This is what constitutes local sociology.

References

Adut, Ari. 2012. "A Theory of the Public Sphere." *Sociological Theory* 30: 238–62.

Alexander, Jeffrey. 2017. *The Drama of Social Life.* Cambridge, UK: Polity.

Alexander, Jeffrey, Bernhard Giesen, Richard Munch, and Neil J. Smelser, eds. 1987. *The Micro–Macro Link.* Berkeley: University of California Press.

Alinsky, Saul. 1971. *Rules for Radicals: A Pragmatic Primer for Realistic Radicals.* New York: Random House.

Allen, Danielle. 2004. *Talking to Strangers: Anxieties of Citizenship since Brown v. Board of Education.* University of Chicago Press.

Allen, Danielle. 2015. "Reconceiving Public Spheres: The Flow Dynamics Model." Pp. 178–207 in Danielle Allen and Jennifer Light, eds., *From Voice to Influence: Understanding Influence in a Digital Age.* University of Chicago Press.

Amann, Peter. 1975. *Revolution and Mass Democracy: The Paris Club Movement in 1948.* Princeton University Press.

Amenta, Edwin. 2007. *Professor Baseball: Searching for Redemption and the Perfect Lineup on the Softball Diamonds of Central Park.* University of Chicago Press.

Anderson, Benedict. 1991. *Imagined Communities.* Revised edition. London: Verso.

Anderson, Elijah. 1979. *A Place on the Corner.* University of Chicago Press.

Anderson, Elijah. 2015. "The White Space." *Sociology of Race and Ethnicity* 1: 1–21.

Andrews, Kenneth, Marshall Ganz, Matt Baggetta, Hahrie Han, and Chaeyoon Lim. 2010. "Leadership, Membership, and Voice: Civic Associations that Work." *American Journal of Sociology* 115: 1191–242.

Ardery, Julia. 1998. *The Temptation: Edgar Tolson and the Genesis of Twentieth-Century Folk Art.* Chapel Hill: University of North Carolina Press.

Aurini, Janice. 2012. "Patterns of Tight and Loose Coupling in a Competitive Marketplace: The Case of Learning Center Franchises." *Sociology of Education* 85: 373–87.

Aveni, Adrian. 1977. "The Not-So-Lonely Crowd: Friendship Groups in Collective Behavior." *Sociometry* 40: 96–9.

Back, Kurt, and Donna Polisar. 1983. "Salons und Kaffeehauser." *Kolner Zeitschrift fur Soziologie und Sozialpsychologie* 25: 276–86.

Baiocchi, Gianpaolo. 2003. "Emergent Public Spheres: Talking Politics in Participatory Governance." *American Sociological Review* 68: 52–74.

Baiocchi, Gianpaolo, Elizabeth Bennett, Alissa Cordner, Peter Klein, and Stephanie Savell. 2014. *The Civic Imagination: Making a Difference in American Political Life.* Boulder, CO: Paradigm.

Bales, Robert Freed. 1950. *Interaction Process Analysis: A Method for the Study of Small Groups.* Cambridge, MA: Addison-Wesley.

Barley, Stephen. 2008. "Coalface Institutionalism." Pp. 490–516 in R. Greenwood, C. Oliver, R. Suddaby, and K. Sahlin-Andersson, eds., *SAGE Handbook of Organizational Institutionalism.* Newbury Park: Sage.

Bartkowski, John. 2000. "Breaking Walls, Raising Fences: Masculinity, Intimacy, and Accountability among the Promise Keepers." *Sociology of Religion* 61: 33–53.

Battilana, Julie. 2006. "Agency and Institutions: The Enabling Role of Individuals' Social Position." *Organization* 13: 653–76.

Battilana, Julie, Bernard Leca, and Eva Boxenbaum. 2009. "How Actors Change Institutions: Towards a Theory of Institutional Entrepreneurship." *Academy of Management Annals* 3: 65–107.

Bearman, Peter S. 1991. "Desertion as Localism: Army Unit

Solidarity and Group Norms in the U.S. Civil War." *Social Forces* 70: 321–42.

Becker, Howard S. 1982. *Art Worlds*. Berkeley: University of California Press.

Becker, Howard S. 1986. *Doing Things Together*. Evanston: Northwestern University Press.

Becker, Howard S., and Blanche Geer. 1960. "Latent Culture: A Note on the Theory of Latent Social Roles." *Administration Science Quarterly* 5: 304–13.

Becker, Howard S., Blanche Geer, and Everett Hughes. 1968. *Making the Grade: The Academic Side of College Life*. New York: Wiley.

Becker, Penny Edgell. 1999. *Congregations in Conflict: Cultural Models of Local Religious Life*. New York: Cambridge University Press.

Bellah, Robert, Richard Madsen, William M. Sullivan, Ann Swidler, and Steven M. Tipton. 1991. *The Good Society*. New York: Knopf.

Benard, Stephen, and Pat Barclay. 2020. "Democratic Competition for Rank, Cooperation, and Deception in Small Groups." *Social Science Quarterly* 101(7): 2423–36.

Bendix, Regina. 1987. "Marmot, Memet and Marmoset: Further Research on the Folklore of Couples." *Western Folklore* 46: 171–91.

Bennett, W. Lance. 2012. "The Personalization of Politics: Political Identity, Social Media, and Changing Patterns of Participation." *Annals, American Academy of Political and Social Science* 644: 20–39.

Benzecry, Claudio. 2011. *The Opera Fanatic: Ethnography of an Obsession*. University of Chicago Press.

Bertaux, Daniel. 1981. *Biography and Society*. Beverly Hills: Sage.

Binder, Amy. 2007. "For Love and Money: Organizations' Creative Responses to Multiple Environmental Logics." *Theory and Society* 36: 547–71.

Bjorklund, Diane. 1985. "Dignified Joking: Humor and Demeanor in a Public Speaking Club." *Symbolic Interaction* 8: 33–46.

Blee, Kathleen. 1992. *Women of the Klan: Racism and Gender in the 1920s*. Berkeley: University of California Press.

Blee, Kathleen. 2012. *Democracy in the Making: How Activist Groups Form*. New York: Oxford University Press.

Blumer, Herbert. 1969. *Symbolic Interactionism: Perspective and Method*. Berkeley: University of California Press.

Bourdieu, Pierre. 1977. *Outline of a Theory of Practice*. Cambridge University Press.

Bourdieu, Pierre. 1984. *Distinction: A Social Critique of the Judgment of Taste*. Cambridge, MA: Harvard University Press.

Bourdieu, Pierre. 1986. "The Forms of Capital." Pp. 46–58 in John Richardson, ed., *Handbook of Theory and Research for the Sociology of Education*. New York: Greenwood Press.

Bourdieu, Pierre. 1991. *Language and Symbolic Power*. Cambridge, MA: Harvard University Press.

Bratman, Michael. 1992. "Shared Cooperative Activity." *Philosophical Review* 101(2): 327–41.

Bratman, Michael. 1993. "Shared Intention." *Ethics* 104(1): 97–113.

Brekhus, Wayne. 2020. *The Sociology of Identity: Authenticity, Multidimensionality, and Mobility*. Cambridge, UK: Polity.

Brint, Steven. 2001. "Gemeinschaft Revisited: A Critique and Reconstruction of the Community Concept." *Sociological Theory* 19: 1–23.

Brissett, Dennis, and Charles Edgley, eds. 2017. *Life as Theater: A Dramaturgical Sourcebook*, 2nd edition. New York: Routledge.

Britton, Marcus. 2008. "'My Regular Spot': Race and Territory in Urban Public Space." *Journal of Contemporary Ethnography* 17: 442–68.

Browning, Christopher, Catherine Calder, Brian Soller, Aubrey Jackson, and Jonathan Dirlam. 2017. "Ecological Networks and Neighborhood Social Organization." *American Journal of Sociology* 122: 1939–88.

Brubaker, Rogers, and Frederick Cooper. 2000. "Beyond 'Identity.'" *Theory and Society* 29: 1–47.

Bryan, Frank M. 2004. *Real Democracy: The New England Town Meeting and How it Works*. University of Chicago Press.

Burke, Peter, and Jan Stets. 1999. "Trust and Commitment through Self-Verification." *Social Psychology Quarterly* 62: 347–66.

Burke, Peter, and Jan Stets. 2009. *Identity Theory*. New York: Oxford University Press.

Burnett, D. Graham. 2001. *A Trial by Jury*. New York: Alfred A. Knopf.

Burt, Ronald. 1992. *Structural Holes: The Social Structure of Competition*. Cambridge, MA: Harvard University Press.

Butler, Judith. 2006. *Gender Trouble: Feminism and the Subversion of Identity*. New York: Routledge.

Calhoun, Craig. 1982. *The Question of Class Struggle: Social Foundations of Popular Radicalism during the Industrial Revolution*. University of Chicago Press.

Campbell, Donald. 1958. "Common Fate, Similarity, and Other Indices of the Status of Aggregates of Persons as Social Entities." *Behavioral Science* 3: 14–25.

Campos-Castillo, Celeste, and Steven Hitlin. 2013. "Copresence: Revisiting a Building Block for Social Interaction Theories." *Sociological Theory* 31: 168–92.

Carley, Kathleen. 1991. "A Theory of Group Stability." *American Sociological Review* 56: 331–54.

Cassell, Joan. 1977. *A Group Called Women: Sisterhood & Symbolism in the Feminist Movement*. New York: David McKay.

Chaves, Mark. 2009. "Congregations' Significance to American Civic Life." Pp. 69–81 in Paul Lichterman and C. Brady Potts, eds., *The Civic Life of American Religion*. Stanford University Press.

Chayko, Mary. 2008. *Portable Communities: The Social Dynamics of Online and Mobile Connectedness*. Albany: SUNY Press.

Chen, Carolyn. 2002. "The Religious Varieties of Ethnic Presence: A Comparison between a Taiwanese Immigrant Buddhist Temple and an Evangelical Christian Church." *Sociology of Religion* 63: 215–38.

Chen, Katherine. 2009. *Enabling Creative Chaos: The Organization behind the Burning Man Event*. University of Chicago Press.

Cherng, Hua-Yu Sebastian, Jessica Calarco, and Grace Kao. 2013. "Along for the Ride: Best Friends' Resources and Adolescents' College Completion." *American Educational Research Journal* 50: 76–106.

Christakis, Nicholas, and James Fowler. 2009. *Connected: How Your Friends' Friends' Friends Affect Everything You Feel, Think, and Do*. Boston: Little, Brown.

Chua, Amy. 2018. *Political Tribes: Group Instinct and the Fate of Nations*. New York: Penguin.

Cockburn, Alexander. 1974. *Idle Passion: Chess and the Dance of Death*. New York: Simon and Schuster.

Coco, Angela, and Ian Woodward. 2007. "Discourses of Authenticity with a Pagan Community." *Journal of Contemporary Ethnography* 36: 479–504.

Coleman, James. 1990. *Foundations of Social Theory*. Cambridge, MA: Harvard University Press.

Collins, Randall. 1999. "Socially Unrecognized Cumulation." *American Sociologist* 30: 41–61.

Collins, Randall. 2004. *Interaction Ritual Chains*. Princeton University Press.

Colomy, Paul. 1998. "Neofunctionalism and Neoinstitutionalism: Human Agency and Interest in Institutional Change." *Sociological Forum* 13(2): 265–300.

Cooley, Charles Horton. 1964 [1902]. *Human Nature and Social Order*. New York: Schocken.

Corte, Ugo. 2013. "A Refinement of Collaborative Circles Theory: Resource Mobilization and Innovation in an Emerging Sport." *Social Psychology Quarterly* 76: 25–51.

Coser, Lewis. 1956. *The Functions of Social Conflict*. New York: Macmillan.

Coser, Lewis. 1974. *Greedy Institutions: Patterns of Undivided Commitment*. New York: Free Press.

Courpasson, David, and Françoise Dany. 2013. "Friends behind the Screen: Enacted Solidarity in the Radicalization of a Blog Protest." Paper presented at the Academy of Management meetings. Orlando, Florida, August.

Cravalho, Mark Andrew. 1996. "Toast on Ice: The Ethnopsychology of the Winter-Over Experience in Antarctica." *Ethos* 24: 628–56.

Crossley, Nick. 2011. *Towards Relational Sociology*. New York: Routledge.

Davis, Murray. 1973. *Intimate Relations*. New York: Free Press.

Dawson, Michael. 1995. *Behind the Mule: Race and Class in African-American Politics*. Princeton University Press.

De La Predelle, Michele. 2006. *Market Day in Provence*. University of Chicago Press.

De Weerd, Marga, and Bert Klandermans. 1999. "Group Identification and Political Protest: Farmers' Protest in the

Netherlands." *European Journal of Social Psychology* 29: 1073–95.

Dégh, Linda, and Andrew Vazsonyi. 1975. "The Hypothesis of Multi-Conduit Transmission in Folklore." Pp. 93–123 in Dan Ben-Amos and Kenneth Goldstein, eds., *Folklore: Performance and Communication*. The Hague: Mouton.

DeLand, Michael. 2018. "The Ocean Run: Stage, Cast, and Performance in a Public Park Basketball Scene." *Journal of Contemporary Ethnography* 47: 28–59.

Della Porta, Donatella. 1988. "Recruitment Processes in Clandestine Political Organizations: Italian Left-wing Terrorism." Pp. 155–69 in Sidney Tarrow, Bert Klandermans, and Hanspeter Kriesi, eds., *From Structure to Action: Comparing Social Movements across Cultures*. New York: JAI Press.

Desmond, Matthew. 2012. "Disposable Ties and the Urban Poor." *American Journal of Sociology* 117: 1295–335.

Desmond, Matthew. 2014. "Relational Ethnography." *Theory & Society* 43: 547–79.

Dewey, John. 1954. *The Public and Its Problems*. Chicago: Swallow Press.

Diamond, Shari, and Mary Rose. 2005. "Real Juries." *Annual Review of Law and Social Science* 1: 255–84.

DiMaggio, Paul. 1988. "Interest and Agency in Institutional Theory." Pp. 3–21 in Lynne Zucker, ed., *Institutional Patterns and Organizations: Culture and Environment*. Cambridge, MA: Ballinger.

DiMaggio, Paul, Eszter Hargittai, W. Russell Neuman, and John Robinson. 2001. "Social Implications of the Internet." *Annual Review of Sociology* 27: 307–36.

Djupe, Paul, and Christopher Gilbert. 2009. *The Political Influences of Churches*. New York: Cambridge University Press.

Donati, Pierpaolo. 2011. *Relational Sociology: A New Paradigm for the Social Sciences*. New York: Routledge.

Donati, Pierpaolo, and Margaret Archer. 2015. *The Relational Subject*. Cambridge University Press.

Dowd, James, and Laura Dowd. 2003. "The Center Holds: From Subculture to Social Worlds." *Teaching Sociology* 31: 20–37.

Dunbar, Robin. 1993. "Coevolution of Neocortex Size, Group

Size, and Language in Humans." *Behavioral Brain Sciences* 16: 681–735.

Duneier, Mitchell. 1999. *Sidewalk*. New York: Farrar, Straus and Giroux.

Durkheim, Émile. 1965 [1912]. *The Elementary Forms of the Religious Life*. New York: Free Press.

Dutton, Jane, and Janet Dukerich. 1991. "Keeping an Eye on the Mirror: Image and Identity in Organizational Adaptation." *Academy of Management Journal* 34: 517–54.

Eliasoph, Nina. 1998. *Avoiding Politics: How Americans Produce Apathy in Everyday Life*. New York: Cambridge University Press.

Eliasoph, Nina. 2012. *Making Volunteers: Civic Life after Welfare's End*. Princeton University Press.

Eliasoph, Nina, and Paul Lichterman. 2003. "Culture in Interaction." *American Journal of Sociology* 108: 735–94.

Ellickson, Robert C. 1991. *Order without Law: How Neighbors Settle Disputes*. Cambridge, MA: Harvard University Press.

Emerson, Robert. 2008. "Responding to Roommate Troubles: Reconsidering Dyadic Control." *Law and Society Review* 42: 483–512.

Emerson, Robert, and Sheldon Messinger. 1977. "The Micro-Politics of Trouble." *Social Problems* 25: 121–34.

Emirbayer, Mustafa, and Mimi Sheller. 1999. "Publics in History." *Theory and Society* 28: 145–97.

Erickson, Karla. 2009. *The Hungry Cowboy: Service and Community in a Neighborhood Restaurant*. Jackson: University of Mississippi Press.

Evans, Sara, and Harry Boyte. 1986. *Free Spaces: The Sources of Democratic Change in America*. New York: Harper & Row.

Everitt, Judson. 2012. "Teacher Careers and Inhabited Institutions: Sense-Making and Arsenals of Teaching Practice in Educational Institutions." *Symbolic Interaction* 35: 203–20.

Farrell, Michael. 2001. *Collaborative Circles: Friendship Dynamics and Creative Work*. University of Chicago Press.

Festinger, Leon, Stanley Schachter, and Kurt Back. 1950. *Social Pressures in Informal Groups: A Study of Human Factors in Housing*. New York: Harper and Row.

Fine, Gary Alan. 1979. "Small Groups and Cultural Creation: The Idioculture of Little League Baseball Teams." *American Sociological Review* 44: 733–45.

Fine, Gary Alan. 1983. *Shared Fantasy: Role-Playing Games as Social Worlds*. University of Chicago Press.

Fine, Gary Alan. 1987. *With the Boys: Little League Baseball and Preadolescent Culture*. University of Chicago Press.

Fine, Gary Alan. 1996. *Kitchens: The Culture of Restaurant Work*. Berkeley: University of California Press.

Fine, Gary Alan. 1998. *Morel Tales: The Culture of Mushrooming*. Cambridge, MA: Harvard University Press.

Fine, Gary Alan. 2001. *Gifted Tongues: High School Debate and Adolescent Culture*. Princeton University Press.

Fine, Gary Alan. 2004. *Everyday Genius: Self-Taught Art and the Culture of Authenticity*. University of Chicago Press.

Fine, Gary Alan. 2007. *Authors of the Storm: Meteorology and the Culture of Prediction*. University of Chicago Press.

Fine, Gary Alan. 2012. *Tiny Publics: A Theory of Group Action and Culture*. New York: Russell Sage Foundation.

Fine, Gary Alan. 2014. "The Hinge: Civil Society, Group Culture, and the Interaction Order." *Social Psychology Quarterly* 77: 5–26.

Fine, Gary Alan. 2015. *Players and Pawns: How Chess Builds Community and Culture*. University of Chicago Press.

Fine, Gary Alan. 2018. *Talking Art: The Culture of Practice and the Practice of Culture in MFA Education*. University of Chicago Press.

Fine, Gary Alan. 2021. *The Hinge: Civil Society, Group Cultures, and the Power of Local Commitments*. University of Chicago Press.

Fine, Gary Alan. In press. *Fair Share: Senior Activism, Tiny Publics, and the Culture of Resistance*. University of Chicago Press.

Fine, Gary Alan, and Tim Hallett. 2014. "Group Cultures and the Everyday Life of Organizations: Interaction Orders and Meso-Analysis." *Organization Studies* 35: 1773–92.

Fine, Gary Alan, and Sherryl Kleinman. 1979. "Rethinking Subculture: An Interactionist Analysis." *American Journal of Sociology* 85: 1–20.

Fine, Gary Alan, and Lisa-Jo Van den Scott. 2011. "Wispy Communities: Transient Gatherings and Imagined Micro-Communities." *American Behavioral Scientist* 55: 1319–35.

Fischer, Claude. 1982. *To Dwell Among Friends: Personal Networks in Town and City*. University of Chicago Press.

Fischer, Claude. 1992. *America Calling: A Social History of the Telephone to 1940*. Berkeley: University of California Press.

Fligstein, Neil. 2001. "Social Skill and the Theory of Fields." *Sociological Theory* 19: 105–25.

Fligstein, Neil, and Doug McAdam. 2012. *A Theory of Fields*. New York: Oxford University Press.

Freeman, Jo. 1972–3. "The Tyranny of Structurelessness." *Berkeley Journal of Sociology* 17: 151–64.

Friedland, Roger, and Robert Alford. 1991. "Bringing Society Back In: Symbols, Practices, and Institutional Contradictions." Pp. 232–63 in Walter Powell and Paul DiMaggio, eds., *The New Institutionalism in Organizational Analysis*. University of Chicago Press.

Friedland, Roger, and John Mohr. 2004. "The Cultural Turn in American Sociology." Pp. 1–70 in Roger Friedland and John Mohr, eds., *Matters of Culture: Cultural Sociology in Practice*. New York: Cambridge University Press.

Furnari, Santi. 2014. "Interstitial Spaces: Microinteraction Settings and the Genesis of New Practices between Institutional Fields." *Academy of Management Review* 39(4): 439–62.

Futrell, Robert, and Pete Simi. 2004. "Free Spaces, Collective Identity, and the Persistence of U.S. White Power Activism." *Social Problems* 51(1): 16–42.

Gamson, William, Bruce Fireman, and Steven Rytina. 1982. *Encounters with Unjust Authority*. Homewood, IL: Dorsey Press.

Gebhardt, Jürgen. 2008. "Friendship, Trust, and Political Order: A Critical Overview." Pp. 315–47 in John von Heyking and Richard Avramenko, eds., *Friendship and Politics: Essays in Political Thought*. University of Notre Dame Press.

Gergen, Kenneth. 1991. *The Saturated Self: Dilemmas of Identity in Everyday Life*. New York: Basic Books.

Gerlach, Luther, and Virginia Hine. 1970. *People, Power, Change: Movements of Social Transformation*. Indianapolis: Bobbs-Merrill.

Geuzendam, Dirk Jan ten. 2006. *The Day Kasparov Quit*. Alkmaar, The Netherlands: New In Chess.

Ghaziani, Amin. 2009. "An 'Amorphous Mist'? The Problem of Measurement in the Study of Culture." *Theory and Society* 38: 581–612.

Gibson, David. 2005. "Taking Turns and Talking Ties: Network

Structure and Conversational Sequences." *American Journal of Sociology* 110: 1561–97.

Gibson, David. 2012. *Talk at the Brink: Deliberation and Decision during the Cuban Missile Crisis.* Princeton University Press.

Gieryn, Thomas. 2018. *Truth Spots: How Places Make People Believe.* University of Chicago Press.

Gieryn, Thomas, and Katherine Oberlin. 2015. "Place and Culture-Making: Geographic Clumping in the Emergence of Artistic Schools." *Poetics* 50: 20–43.

Giesen, Bernhard. 2001. "Cosmopolitans, Patriots, Jacobins, and Romantics." Pp. 221–50 in Shmuel N. Eisenstadt, Wolfgang Schluchter, and Bjorn Wittrock, eds., *Public Spheres and Collective Identities.* New Brunswick, NJ: Transaction.

Gilbert, Margaret. 1997. "What Is It for Us to Intend?" *Synthese Library*: 65–86.

Gilbert, Margaret. 2009. "Shared Intentions and Personal Intentions." *Philosophical Studies* 144: 167–87.

Glassberg, David. 1990. *American Historical Pageantry: The Uses of Tradition in the Early Twentieth Century.* Chapel Hill: University of North Carolina Press.

Goffman, Erving. 1959. *The Presentation of Self in Everyday Life.* New York: Anchor.

Goffman, Erving. 1967. *Interaction Ritual: Essays on Face-to-Face Behavior.* New York: Anchor.

Goffman, Erving. 1974. *Frame Analysis: An Essay in the Organization of Experience.* Cambridge, MA: Harvard University Press.

Goffman, Erving. 1983. "The Interaction Order." *American Sociological Review* 48: 1–17.

Goldfarb, Jeffrey. 2006. *The Politics of Small Things: The Power of the Powerless in Dark Times.* University of Chicago Press.

Goodman, Dena. 1994. *The Republic of Letters: A Cultural History of the French Enlightenment.* Ithaca, NY: Cornell University Press.

Goodwin, Jeff. 1997. "The Libidinal Constitution of a High-Risk Social Movement: Affectual Ties and Solidarity in the Huk Rebellion, 1946 to 1954." *American Sociological Review* 62: 53–69.

Gordon, Linda. 2017. *The Second Coming of the KKK: The Ku*

Klux Klan of the 1920s and the American Political Tradition. New York: Liveright.

Gould, Roger V. 1995. *Insurgent Identities: Class, Community, and Protest in Paris from 1848 to the Commune.* University of Chicago Press.

Grannis, Rick. 2009. *From the Ground Up: Translating Geography into Community through Neighbor Networks.* Princeton University Press.

Granovetter, Mark. 1973. "The Strength of Weak Ties." *American Journal of Sociology* 78: 1360–80.

Granovetter, Mark. 1974. *Getting a Job: A Study of Contacts and Careers.* Cambridge, MA: Harvard University Press.

Greene, Joshua. 2013. *Moral Tribes: Emotion, Reason, and the Gap between Us and Them.* New York: Penguin.

Guhin, Jeffrey. 2016. "Why Worry about Evolution? Boundaries, Practices, and Moral Salience in Sunni and Evangelical High Schools." *Sociological Theory* 34: 151–74.

Gusfield, Joseph. 1963. *Symbolic Crusade: Status Politics and the American Temperance Movement.* Urbana: University of Illinois Press.

Habermas, Jürgen. 1989. *The Structural Transformation of the Public Sphere: An Inquiry into a Category of Bourgeois Society,* translated by Thomas Burger. Cambridge, MA: MIT Press.

Hackman, J. Richard, and Nancy Katz. 2010. "Group Behavior and Performance." Pp. 1208–51 in Susan Fiske, Daniel Gilbert, and Gardner Lindzey, eds., *Handbook of Social Psychology,* fifth edition. New York: Wiley.

Haedicke, Michael. 2012. "'Keeping our Mission, Changing our System': Translation and Organizational Change in Natural Foods Co-ops." *Sociological Quarterly* 53: 44–67.

Haley, Alex. 1964. *The Autobiography of Malcolm X.* New York: Ballantine Books.

Hall, Peter M. 1972. "A Symbolic Interactionist Analysis of Politics." *Sociological Inquiry* 42: 35–75.

Hallett, Tim. 2003. "Symbolic Power and Organizational Culture." *Sociological Theory* 21: 128–49.

Hallett, Tim. 2007. "Between Deference and Distinction: Interaction Ritual through Symbolic Power in an Educational Institution." *Social Psychology Quarterly* 70: 148–71.

Hallett, Tim. 2010. "The Myth Incarnate: Recoupling Processes,

Turmoil, and Inhabited Institutions in an Urban Elementary School." *American Sociological Review* 75: 52–74.

Hallett, Tim, and Matt Gougherty. 2018. "Professional Education in the University Context: Toward an Inhabited Institutional View of Socialization." Pp. 144–80 in Jal Mehta and Scott Davies, eds., *Education in a New Society: Renewing the Sociology of Education.* University of Chicago Press.

Hallett, Tim, Brent Harger, and Donna Eder. 2009. "Gossip at Work: Unsanctioned Evaluative Talk in Formal School Meetings." *Journal of Contemporary Ethnography* 38: 584–618.

Hallett, Tim, and Amelia Hawbaker. 2020. "Bringing Society Back In Again: The Importance of Social Interaction in an Inhabited Institutionalism." *Research in the Sociology of Organizations* 65: 317–36.

Hallett, Tim, and Amelia Hawbaker. 2021. "The Case for an Inhabited Institutionalism in Organizational Research: Interaction, Coupling, and Change Reconsidered." *Theory and Society* 50: 1–32.

Hallett, Tim, and Marc Ventresca. 2006. "Inhabited Institutions: Social Interaction and Organizational Forms in Gouldner's *Patterns of Industrial Bureaucracy.*" *Theory and Society* 35: 213–36.

Harding, David. 2010. *Living the Drama: Community, Conflict and Culture among Inner-City Boys.* University of Chicago Press.

Hardy, Cynthia, and Steve Maguire. 2008. "Institutional Entrepreneurship." Pp. 198–217 in Royston Greenwood, Christine Oliver, Roy Suddaby, and Kirsten Sahlin-Andersson, eds., *SAGE Handbook of Organizational Institutionalism.* Thousand Oaks, CA: Sage.

Harper, Douglas. 2001. *Changing Works: Visions of a Lost Agriculture.* University of Chicago Press.

Harrington, Brooke. 2008. *Pop Finance: Investment Clubs and the New Investor Populism.* Princeton University Press.

Hart, Stephen. 2001. *Cultural Dilemmas of Progressive Politics.* University of Chicago Press.

Haug, Christoph. 2013. "Organizing Spaces: Meeting Arenas as a Social Movement Infrastructure between Organization, Network, and Institution." *Organization Studies* 34(5–6): 705–32.

Hebb, Donald O. 1974. "What Psychology Is About." *American Psychologist* 29: 71–87.

Helguera, Pablo. 2012. *Art Scenes: The Social Scripts of the Art World*. New York: Jorge Pinto Books.

Herzfeld, Michael. 1993. *The Social Production of Indifference: Exploring the Symbolic Roots of Western Bureaucracy*. University of Chicago Press.

Hillmann, Henning. 2008. "Localism and the Limits of Political Brokerage: Evidence from Revolutionary Vermont." *American Journal of Sociology* 114: 287–331.

Hoffman, Paul. 2007. *King's Gambit: A Son, A Father, and the World's Most Dangerous Game*. New York: Hyperion.

Hogg, Michael, Dominic Abrams, Sabine Otten, and Steve Hinkle. 2004. "The Social Identity Perspective: Intergroup Relations, Self-Conception, and Small Groups." *Small Group Research* 35: 246–76.

Hogg, Michael, Deborah Terry, and Katherine White. 1995. "A Tale of Two Theories: A Critical Comparison of Identity Theory and Social Identity Theory." *Social Psychology Quarterly* 58: 255–69.

Hollingshead, August B. 1939. "Behavior Systems as a Field for Research." *American Sociological Review* 4: 816–22.

Honohan, Isault. 2001. "Friends, Strangers or Countrymen? The Ties between Citizens as Colleagues." *Political Studies* 49: 51–69.

House, James. 1981. "Social Structure and Personality." Pp. 525–61 in Morris Rosenberg and Ralph Turner, eds., *Social Psychology: Sociological Perspectives*. New York: Basic Books.

Ignatow, Gabe. 2004. "Speaking Together, Thinking Together? Exploring Metaphor and Cognition in a Shipyard Union Dispute." *Sociological Forum* 19: 405–33.

Ikegami, Eiko. 2000. "A Sociological Theory of Publics: Identity and Culture as Emergent Properties in Networks." *Social Research* 67: 989–1029.

Ikegami, Eiko. 2005. *Bonds of Civility: Aesthetic Networks and the Political Origins of Japanese Culture*. New York: Cambridge University Press.

Janis, Irving. 1972. *Victims of Groupthink: A Psychological Study of Foreign-Policy Decisions and Fiascoes*. Boston: Houghton Mifflin.

Jasper, James. 2004. "A Strategic Approach to Collective Action: Looking for Agency in Social-Movement Choices." *Mobilization* 9: 1–16.

Jasper, James. 2010. "Social Movement Theory Today: Toward a Theory of Action?" *Sociology Compass* 10: 965–76.

Jasper, James, and Frédéric Volpi. 2018. "Introduction: Rethinking Mobilization after the Arab Uprisings." Pp. 11–40 in Frédéric Volpi and James Jasper, eds., *Microfoundations of the Arab Uprisings: Mapping Interactions between Regimes and Protesters*. Amsterdam University Press.

Jepperson, Ronald, and John Meyer. 2011. "Multiple Levels of Analysis and the Limitations of Methodological Individualisms." *Sociological Theory* 29: 54–73.

Johnston, Hank. 2006. "'Let's Get Small': The Dynamics of (Small) Contention in Repressive States." *Mobilization* 11: 195–212.

Junger, Sebastian. 2016. *Tribe: On Homecoming and Belonging*. New York: Twelve.

Kaplan, Danny. 2018. *The Nation as Social Club: Building Solidarity through Sociability*. New York: Palgrave Macmillan.

Katovich, Michael, and Carl Couch. 1992. "The Nature of Social Pasts and Their Uses as Foundations for Situated Action." *Symbolic Interaction* 15: 25–48.

Katz, Nancy, David Lazer, Holly Arrow, and Noshir Contractor. 2004. "Network Theory and Small Groups." *Small Group Research* 35: 207–32.

Kaufman, Jason. 1999. "Three Views of Associationalism in Nineteenth-Century America: An Empirical Examination." *American Journal of Sociology* 104: 1296–1345.

Kaufmann, Jean-Claude. 2009. *Gripes: The Little Quarrels of Couples*. Cambridge, UK: Polity.

Keohane, Nannerl. 2014. "Civil Society and Good Democratic Leadership." Unpublished manuscript, Princeton University.

Kipling, Rudyard. 1919. *Rudyard Kipling's Verse*. New York: Doubleday Page.

Kitts, James. 2000. "Mobilizing in Black Boxes: Social Networks and Participation in Social Movement Organizations." *Mobilization* 5: 241–57.

Klandermans, Bert. 1997. *The Social Psychology of Protest*. Oxford: Blackwell.

Klinenberg, Eric. 2012. *Going Solo: The Extraordinary Rise and Surprising Appeal of Living Alone*. New York: Penguin.

Koselleck, Reinhart. 1988. *Critique and Crisis: Enlightenment and the Pathogenesis of Modern Society*. Cambridge, MA: MIT Press.

Kuhn, Manford, and Thomas McPartland. 1954. "An Empirical Investigation of Self-Attitudes." *American Sociological Review* 19: 68–76.

Kuzmics, Helmut. 1991. "Embarrassment and Civilization: On Some Similarities and Differences in the Work of Goffman and Elias." *Theory, Culture, and Society* 8: 1–30.

Lahire, Bernard. 2011. *The Plural Actor*. Cambridge, UK: Polity.

Lane, Christel. 1981. *The Rites of Rulers: Ritual in Industrial Society – The Soviet Case*. Cambridge University Press.

Lanier-Vos, Dan. 2014. "Israel in the Poconos: Simulating the Nation in a Jewish-American Summer Camp." *Theory and Society* 43(1): 91–116.

Latour, Bruno. 2005. *Reassembling the Social: An Introduction to Actor–Network Theory*. New York: Oxford University Press.

Laumann, Edward. 1973. *Bonds of Pluralism: The Form and Substance of Urban Social Networks*. New York: Wiley.

Lawler, Edward, Shane R. Thye, and Jeongkoo Yoon. 2009. *Social Commitments in a Depersonalized World*. New York: Russell Sage Foundation.

Lawrence, Tom, and Roy Suddaby. 2006. "Institutions and Institutional Work." Pp. 215–54 in Stewart Clegg, Cynthia Hardy, Tom Lawrence, and Walter Nord, eds., *Handbook of Organization Studies*, 2nd edition. London: Sage.

Levine, John, and Richard Moreland. 1994. "Group Socialization: Theory and Research." *European Review of Social Psychology* 5: 305–36.

Lichterman, Paul. 2005. *Elusive Togetherness: Church Groups Trying to Bridge America's Divisions*. Princeton University Press.

Liebow, Elliot. 1967. *Tally's Corner: A Study of Negro Streetcorner Men*. Boston: Little, Brown.

Lim, Chaeyoon, and Robert Putnam. 2010. "Religion, Social Networks, and Subjective Well-Being." *American Sociological Review* 75: 914–33.

Lipman-Blumen, Jean, and Harold Leavitt. 2001. *Hot Groups: Seeding Them, Feeding Them, and Using Them to Ignite Your Organization*. New York: Oxford University Press.

Lipsky, Michael. 2010. *Street-Level Bureaucracy: Dilemmas of the Individual in Public Service, 30th Anniversary Expanded Edition*. New York: Russell Sage Foundation.

List, Christian, and Philip Pettit. 2011. *Group Agency: The Possibility, Design, and Status of Corporate Agents*. Oxford University Press.

Lizardo, Omar. 2006. "Cultural Tastes and Personal Networks." *American Sociological Review* 71: 778–807.

Lofland, John, and Michael Jamison. 1984. "Social Movement Locals: Modal Member Structures." *Sociological Analysis* 45: 115–29.

Long, Elizabeth. 2003. *Book Clubs: Women and the Uses of Reading in Everyday Life*. University of Chicago Press.

Lorenz, Taylor, Kellen Browning, and Sheera Frenkel. 2020. "TikTok Teens and K-Pop Fans Say They Sank Trump Rally." *New York Times* (June 21): www.nytimes.com/2020/06/21/style/tiktok-trump-rally-tulsa.html.

Lukes, Steven. 2005. *Power: A Radical View*. 2nd edition. New York: Palgrave Macmillan.

McAdam, Doug. 1988. *Freedom Summer*. New York: Oxford University Press.

McAdam, Doug, and Ronnelle Paulsen. 1993. "Specifying the Relationship between Social Ties and Activism." *American Journal of Sociology* 99: 640–67.

McCabe, Janice. 2016. *Connecting in College: How Friendship Networks Matter for Academic and Social Success*. University of Chicago Press.

McCarthy, John, and Mayer Zald. 1977. "Resource Mobilization and Social Movements: A Partial Theory." *Ameriaca Journal of Sociology* 82(6): 1212–41.

McFeat, Tom. 1974. *Small-Group Cultures*. New York: Pergamon.

McGinty, Patrick. 2014. "Divided and Drifting: Interactionism and the Neglect of Social Organizational Analysis in Organization Studies." *Symbolic Interaction* 37: 155–86.

McLeod, Jane, and Kathryn Lively. 2003. "Social Structure and Personality." Pp. 77–102 in John Delamater (ed.), *Handbook of Social Psychology*. New York: Springer.

MacNeil, Mark, and Muzafer Sherif. 1976. "Norm Change over Subject Generations as a Function of Arbitrariness of Prescribed Norms." *Journal of Personality and Social Psychology* 34: 762–73.

McPhail, Clark. 1991. *The Myth of the Madding Crowd*. New York: Aldine.

McPherson, Miller, and Lynn Smith-Lovin. 1987. "Homophily

in Voluntary Organizations: Status Distance and the Composition of Face-to-Face Groups." *American Sociological Review* 52: 370–9.

McPherson, Miller, Lynn Smith-Lovin, and Matthew Brashears. 2006. "Social Isolation in America: Changes in Core Discussion Networks over Two Decades." *American Sociological Review* 71: 353–75.

Maffesoli, Michel. 1996. *The Time of the Tribes: The Decline of Individualism in Mass Society.* Thousand Oaks, CA: Sage.

Maines, David. 1977. "Social Organization and Social Structure in Symbolic Interactionist Thought." *Annual Review of Sociology* 3: 235–59.

Maines, David. 1999. "Information Pools and Racialized Narrative Structures." *Sociological Quarterly* 40: 316–26.

Maines, David, Noreen Sugrue, and Michael Katovich. 1983. "The Sociological Import of G. H. Mead's Theory of the Past." *American Sociological Review* 48: 161–73.

Mansbridge, Jane. 1980. *Beyond Adversary Democracy.* New York: Basic Books.

Martin, Joanne. 1992. *Culture in Organizations: Three Perspectives.* New York: Oxford University Press.

Mead, George Herbert. 1934. *Mind, Self, and Society: From the Standpoint of a Social Behaviorist.* University of Chicago Press.

Mechling, Jay. 2001. *On My Honor: Boy Scouts and the Making of American Youth.* University of Chicago Press.

Melucci, Alberto. 1989. *Nomads of the Present: Social Movements and Individual Needs in Contemporary Society.* Philadelphia: Temple University Press.

Menchik, Daniel A. 2019. "Tethered Venues: Discerning Distant Influences on a Field Site." *Sociological Methods and Research* 48: 850–76.

Messinger, Sheldon. 1955. "Organizational Transformation: A Case Study of a Declining Social Movement." *American Sociological Review* 20: 3–10.

Meyer, John, and Ronald Jepperson. 2000. "The 'Actors' of Modern Society: The Cultural Construction of Social Agency." *Sociological Theory* 18: 100–20.

Meyer, John, and Brian Rowan. 1977. "Institutionalized Organizations: Formal Structure as Myth and Ceremony." *American Journal of Sociology* 83(2): 340–63.

Meyer, Robinson. 2013. "It's a Lonely World." *The Atlantic* (December 19): www.theatlantic.com/technology/archive/2013/12/its-a-lonely-world-the-median-twitter-user-has-1-measly-follower/282513.

Milgram, Stanley. 1967. "The Small-World Problem." *Psychology Today* 1(May): 62–7.

Mische, Ann, and Harrison White. 1998. "Between Conversation and Situation: Public Switching Dynamics across Network-Domains." *Social Research* 65: 295–324.

Misztal, Barbara. 2001. "Normality and Trust in Goffman's Theory of Interaction Order." *Sociological Theory* 19: 312–24.

Morrill, Calvin. 1995. *The Executive Way: Conflict Management in Corporations.* University of Chicago Press.

Morrill, Calvin. 2008. "Culture and Organization Theory." *Annals of the American Academy of Political and Social Science* 613: 15–40.

Muggleton, David. 2000. *Inside Subculture: The Postmodern Meaning of Style.* Oxford: Berg.

Mullins, Nicholas. 1973. *Theories and Theory Groups in Contemporary American Sociology.* New York: Harper & Row.

Munch, Richard, and Neil Smelser. 1993. *Theory of Culture.* Berkeley: University of California Press.

Nunn, Lisa. 2014. *Defining Student Success: The Role of School and Culture.* New Brunswick: Rutgers University Press.

Oldenburg, Ray. 1989. *The Great Good Place.* St. Paul: Paragon House.

Olson, Mancur. 1965. *The Logic of Collective Action: Public Goods and the Theory of Groups.* Cambridge, MA: Harvard University Press.

Oring, Elliott. 1984. "Dyadic Traditions." *Journal of Folklore Research* 21: 19–28.

Ouchi, William, and Alan Wilkins. 1985. "Organizational Culture." *Annual Review of Sociology* 11: 457–83.

Parker, John, and Edward Hackett. 2012. "Hot Spots and Hot Moments in Scientific Collaborations and Social Movements." *American Sociological Review* 77: 21–44.

Patrick, Brian. 2006. "Group Ethos and the Communication of Social Action." *Small Group Research* 37(5): 925–58.

Perrin, Andrew. 2005. "Political Microcultures: Linking Civic Life and Democratic Discourse." *Social Forces* 84: 1049–82.

Perry, Brea, and Bernice Pescosolido. 2015. "Social Network Activation: The Role of Health Discussion Partners in Recovery from Mental Illness." *Social Science and Medicine* 125(1): 116–28.

Pescosolido, Bernice. 1992. "Beyond Rational Choice: The Social Dynamics of How People Seek Help." *American Journal of Sociology* 94(4): 1096–138.

Peterson, Richard, and Roger Kern. 1996. "Changing Highbrow Taste: From Snob to Omnivore." *American Sociological Review* 61: 900–7.

Pettigrew, Thomas. 1967. "Social Evaluation Theory: Convergences and Applications." Pp. 241–311 in David Levine, ed., *Nebraska Symposium on Motivation, 1967*. Lincoln: University of Nebraska Press.

Pfaff, Steven. 1996. "Collective Identity and Informal Groups in Revolutionary Mobilization: East Germany in 1989." *Social Forces* 75: 91–118.

Polletta, Francesca. 2002. *Freedom Is an Endless Meeting: Democracy in American Social Movements*. University of Chicago Press.

Polletta, Francesca, and James Jasper. 2001. "Collective Identity and Social Movements." *Annual Review of Sociology* 27: 283–305.

Portes, Alejandro. 1998. "Social Capital: Its Origins and Applications in Modern Sociology." *Annual Review of Sociology* 24: 1–24.

Powell, Brian, Catherine Bolzendahl, Claudia Geist, and Lala Carr Steelman. 2010. *Counted Out: Same-Sex Relations and Americans' Definitions of Family*. New York: Russell Sage Foundation.

Powell, Walter W., and Jeannette Colyvas. 2008. "Microfoundations of Institutional Theory." Pp. 276–98 in R. Greenwood, C. Oliver, R. Suddaby, and K. Sahlin-Andersson, eds., *The SAGE Handbook of Organizational Institutionalism*. Newbury Park: Sage.

Prus, Robert, and Styllianos Irini. 1980. *Hookers, Rounders and Desk Clerks: The Social Organization of the Hotel Community*. New York: Forkner Publishing Company.

Putnam, Robert. 1995. "Tuning In, Tuning Out: The Strange Disappearance of Social Capital in America." *PS: Political Science and Politics* 28: 664–83.

Putnam, Robert. 2000. *Bowling Alone: The Collapse and Revival of American Community*. New York: Simon and Schuster.

Putnam, Robert, and David Campbell. 2010. *American Grace: How Religion Divides and Unites Us*. New York: Simon and Schuster.

Quillian, Lincoln, and Devah Pager. 2001. "Black Neighbors, Higher Crime? The Role of Racial Stereotypes in Evaluations of Neighborhood Crime." *American Journal of Sociology* 107: 717–67.

Rawlings, Craig. 2020. "Cognitive Authority and the Constraint of Attitude Change in Groups." *American Sociological Review* 85: 992–1021.

Reed, Isaac. 2006. "Social Dramas, Shipwrecks, and Cockfights: Conflict and Complicity in Social Performance." Pp. 146–68 in Jeffrey Alexander, Bernhard Giesen, and Jason Mast, eds., *Social Performance: Symbolic Action, Cultural Pragmatics and Ritual*. Cambridge University Press.

Reed, Isaac. 2017. "Chains of Power and Their Representation." *Sociological Theory* 35: 87–117.

Reedy, Justin, John Gastil, and Michael Gabbay. 2013. "Terrorism and Small Groups: An Analytic Framework for Group Disruption." *Small Group Research* 44: 599–626.

Reger, Jo. 2002. "Organizational Dynamics and Construction of Multiple Feminist Identities in the National Organization for Women." *Gender & Society* 16: 710–27.

Ricoeur, Paul. 1984. *Time and Narrative*. University of Chicago Press.

Riley, Anna, and Peter Burke. 1995. "Identities and Self-Verification in the Small Group." *Social Psychology Quarterly* 58: 61–73.

Riley, Dylan. 2010. *The Civic Foundations of Fascism in Europe: Italy, Spain, and Romania, 1870–1945*. Baltimore: Johns Hopkins University Press.

Robnett, Belinda. 1996. "African-American Women in the Civil Rights Movement, 1954–1965: Gender, Leadership, and Micromobilization." *American Journal of Sociology* 101: 1661–93.

Rose, Edward, and William Felton. 1955. "Experimental Histories of Culture." *American Sociological Review* 20: 382–92.

Ruiz-Junco, Natalia, and Baptiste Brossard. 2019. *Updating*

Charles H. Cooley: Contemporary Perspectives on a Sociological Classic. New York: Routledge.

Sacks, Harvey. 1995. *Lectures on Conversation.* Malden, MA: Wiley-Blackwell.

Sageman, Marc. 2008. *Leaderless Jihad: Terror Networks in the Twenty-First Century.* Philadelphia: University of Pennsylvania Press.

Sampson, Robert J., Jeffrey Morenoff, and Felton Earls. 1999. "Spatial Dynamics of Collective Efficacy for Children." *American Sociological Review* 64: 633–60.

Sampson, Robert J., Jeffrey Morenoff, and Thomas Gannon-Rowley. 2002. "Assessing Neighborhood Effects: Social Processes and New Directions in Research." *Annual Review of Sociology* 28: 443–78.

Sampson, Robert J., and Stephen Raudenbush. 1999. "Systematic Social Observation of Public Spaces: A New Look at Disorder in Urban Neighborhoods." *American Journal of Sociology* 105: 603–51.

Sato, Ikuya. 1991. *Kamikaze Biker: Parody and Anomy in Affluent Japan.* University of Chicago Press.

Sawyer, R. Keith. 2005. *Social Emergence: Societies as Complex Systems.* New York: Cambridge University Press.

Schegloff, Emanuel. 1992. "Repair after Next Turn: The Last Structurally Provided Defense of Intersubjectivity in Conversation." *American Journal of Sociology* 97: 1295–345.

Schegloff, Emanuel. 2007. *Sequence Organization in Interaction,* Vol. I: *A Primer in Conversation Analysis.* Cambridge University Press.

Schnettler, Sebastian. 2009. "A Structured Overview of Fifty Years of Small-World Research." *Social Networks* 31: 165–78.

Schutz, Alfred. 1967. *The Phenomenology of the Social World.* Evanston: Northwestern University Press.

Scott, James. 1987. *Weapons of the Weak: Everyday Forms of Peasant Resistance.* New Haven: Yale University Press.

Scott, James. 2012. *Two Cheers for Anarchism.* Princeton University Press.

Scott, Marvin B., and Stanford Lyman. 1968. "Accounts." *American Sociological Review* 33: 46–62.

Scully, Maureen, and Douglass Creed. 1997. "Stealth Legitimacy: Employee Activism and Corporate Response during the

Diffusion of Domestic Partner Benefits." Paper presented at the Academy of Management Meetings. Boston.

Selznick, Philip. 1966 [1949]. *TVA and the Grass Roots*. New York: Harper and Row.

Sennett, Richard. 2012. *Together: The Rituals, Pleasures, and Politics of Cooperation*. New Haven: Yale University Press.

Sherif, Muzafer, O. J. Harvey, B. J. Hood, and Carolyn W. Sherif. 1961. *Intergroup Conflict and Cooperation: The Robbers Cave Experiment*. Norman: University of Oklahoma Book Exchange.

Sherif, Muzafer, and Carolyn Sherif. 1964. *Reference Groups*. Chicago: Regnery.

Shibutani, Tamotsu. 1955. "Reference Groups as Perspectives." *American Journal of Sociology* 60: 562–9.

Silver, Daniel, Terry Nichols Clark, and Clemente Jesus Navarro Yanez. 2010. "Scenes: Social Context in an Age of Contingency." *Social Forces* 88: 2293–324.

Simmel, Georg. 1950. *The Sociology of Georg Simmel*, translated and edited by Kurt Wolff. New York: Free Press.

Sion, Liora, and Eyal Ben-Ari. 2005. "'Weary, Hungry and Horny': Humour and Laughter in Israel's Military Reserves." *Israel Affairs* 11: 656–72.

Sklair, Leslie. 1973. *Organized Knowledge: Sociological View of Science and Technology*. London: Hart-Davis MacGibbon.

Sloan, Melissa. 2007. "The 'Real Self' and Inauthenticity: The Importance of Self-Concept Anchorage for Emotional Experiences in the Workplace." *Social Psychology Quarterly* 70: 305–18.

Small, Mario. 2004. *Villa Victoria: The Transformation of Social Capital in a Boston Barrio*. University of Chicago Press.

Small, Mario. 2009. *Unanticipated Gains: Origins of Network Inequality in Everyday Life*. New York: Oxford University Press.

Smelser, Neil. 1962. *Theory of Collective Behavior*. New York: Free Press.

Smith, Gregory. 2006. *Erving Goffman*. Abingdon, UK: Routledge.

Snow, David, Daniel Cress, Liam Downey, and Andrew Jones. 1998. "Disrupting the Quotidian: Reconceptualizing the Relationship between Breakdown and the Emergence of Collective Action." *Mobilization* 3: 1–22.

Snow, David, and Dana Moss. 2014. "Protest on the Fly: Toward a Theory of Spontaneity in the Dynamics of Protest and Social Movements." *American Sociological Review* 79: 1122–43.

Snow, David, Louis Zurcher, and Sheldon Ekland-Olsen. 1980. "Social Networks and Social Movements: A Microstructural Approach to Differential Recruitment." *American Sociological Review* 45: 787–801.

Sparrowe, Raymond, Robert Liden, Sandy Wayne, and Maria Kraimer. 2001. "Social Networks and the Performance of Individuals and Groups." *Academy of Management Journal* 44: 316–25.

Spector, Malcolm. 1973. "Secrecy in Job Seeking among Government Attorneys: Two Contingencies in the Theory of Subcultures." *Urban Life and Culture* 2: 211–29.

Stebbins, Robert. 2006. *Serious Leisure: A Perspective for Our Time*. New Brunswick, NJ: Transaction.

Steiner, Ivan. 1974. "Whatever Happened to the Group in Social Psychology?" *Journal of Experimental Social Psychology* 10: 94–108.

Stets, Jan, and Alicia Cast. 2007. "Resources and Identity Verification from an Identity Theory Perspective." *Sociological Perspectives* 50: 517–43.

Strauss, Anselm. 1978. *Negotiations: Varieties, Contexts, Processes and Social Order*. San Francisco: Jossey-Bass.

Stryker, Sheldon. 1980. *Symbolic Interactionism: A Social Structural Version*. Menlo Park, CA: Benjamin/Cummings.

Stryker, Sheldon, and Peter Burke. 2000. "The Past, Present, and Future of an Identity Theory." *Social Psychology Quarterly* 63: 284–97.

Stryker, Sheldon, and Richard Serpe. 1994. "Identity Salience and Psychological Centrality: Equivalent, Overlapping, or Complementary Concepts?" *Social Psychology Quarterly* 57: 16–35.

Summers-Effler, Erika. 2010. *Laughing Saints and Righteous Heroes: Emotional Rhythms in Social Movement Groups*. University of Chicago Press.

Swidler, Ann. 1986. "Culture in Action: Symbols and Strategies." *American Sociological Review* 51: 273–86.

Tajfel, Henri. 1982. *Social Identity and Intergroup Behavior*. Cambridge University Press.

Tajfel, Henri, Michael Billig, R. P. Bundy, and C. Flament. 1971. "Social Categorization and Intergroup Behavior." *European Journal of Social Psychology* 1: 149–77.

Tavory, Iddo. 2016. *Summoned: Identification and Religious Life in a Jewish Neighborhood.* University of Chicago Press.

Tavory, Iddo, and Gary Alan Fine. 2020. "Disruption and the Theory of the Interaction Order." *Theory & Society* 49: 365–85.

Tilly, Charles. 1996. "Invisible Elbow." *Sociological Forum* 11: 589–601.

Tocqueville, Alexis de. 1966 [1835]. *Democracy in America.* New York: Harper and Row.

Toennies, Ferdinand. 2001 [1887]. *Community and Civil Society,* translated by Jose Harris and Margaret Hollis. Cambridge University Press.

Tuomela, Raimo. 2007. *The Philosophy of Sociality: The Shared Point of View.* New York: Oxford University Press.

Turner, John, Michael Hogg, Penelope Oakes, Stephen Reicher, and Margaret Wetherell. 1987. *Rediscovering the Social Group: A Self-Categorization Theory.* Oxford: Blackwell.

Turner, Jonathan. 2005. "A New Approach for Theoretically Integrating Micro and Macro Analysis." Pp. 404–22 in Craig Calhoun, Chris Rojek, and Brian Turner, eds., *The SAGE Handbook of Sociology.* London: Sage.

Turner, Jonathan, and David Boyns. 2002. "The Return of Grand Theory." Pp. 353–78 in Jonathan Turner, ed., *Handbook of Sociological Theory.* New York: Plenum Publishers.

Uzzi, Brian. 1996. "The Sources and Consequences of Embeddedness for the Economic Performance of Organizations: The Network Effect." *American Sociological Review* 61: 674–98.

Vaisey, Stephen. 2009. "Motivation and Justification: A Dual-Process Model of Culture in Action." *American Journal of Sociology* 114: 1675–715.

Vaisey, Stephen, and Omar Lizardo. 2010. "Can Cultural Worldviews Influence Network Composition?" *Social Forces* 88: 1595–618.

Waitzkin, Fred. 1988. *Searching for Bobby Fischer: The World of Chess Observed by the Father of a Child Prodigy.* New York: Random House.

Walsh, Katherine Cramer. 2003. *Talking about Politics: Informal Groups and Social Identity in American Life.* University of Chicago Press.

Walzer, Michael. 1992. "The Civil Society Argument." Pp. 89–107 in Chantal Mouffe, ed., *Dimensions of Radical Democracy: Pluralism, Citizenship, Community*. London: Verso.

Warner, W. Lloyd. 1953. *The Living and the Dead*. New Haven: Yale University Press.

Watts, Duncan. 1999. *Small Worlds: The Dynamics of Networks between Order and Randomness*. Princeton University Press.

Weeks, John. 2003. *Unpopular Culture: The Ritual of Complaint in a British Bank*. University of Chicago Press.

Weick, Karl. 1995. *Sensemaking in Organizations*. Thousand Oaks, CA: Sage.

White, Harrison. 1995. "Network Switchings and Bayesian Forks: Reconstructing the Social and Behavioral Sciences." *Social Research* 62: 1035–63.

Whittier, Nancy. 1997. "Political Generations, Micro-Cohorts, and the Transformation of Social Movements." *American Sociological Review* 62: 760–78.

Whyte, Martin King. 1974. *Small Groups and Political Rituals in China*. Berkeley: University of California Press.

Whyte, William F. 1943. *Street Corner Society*. University of Chicago Press.

Wiley, Juniper. 1991. "A Refracted Reality of Everyday Life: The Constructed Culture of a Therapeutic Community." *Symbolic Interaction* 14(2): 139–63.

Wilkins, Amy. 2008. *Wannabes, Goths, and Christians: The Boundaries of Sex, Style, and Status*. University of Chicago Press.

Wuthnow, Robert. 1994. *Sharing the Journey: Support Groups and America's New Quest for Community*. New York: Free Press.

Wuthnow, Robert. 1998. *Loose Connections: Joining Together in America's Fragmented Communities*. Cambridge, MA: Harvard University Press.

Zerubavel, Eviatar. 1997. *Social Mindscapes: An Introduction to Cognitive Sociology*. Cambridge, MA: Harvard University Press.

Zhao, Dingxin. 2001. *The Power of Tiananmen: State–Society Relations and the 1989 Beijing Student Movement*. University of Chicago Press.

Znaniecki, Florian. 1940. *The Social Role of the Man of Knowledge*. New York: Columbia University Press.

Zuboff, Shoshana. 1988. *In the Age of the Smart Machine: The Future of Work and Power.* New York: Basic Books.

Zurcher, Louis. 1977. *The Mutable Self.* Beverly Hills: Sage.

Zweigenhaft, Richard, and William Domhoff. 2006. *Diversity in the Power Elite: How It Happened and Why It Matters.* New York: Rowman and Littlefield.

Index